Lifewriting
Learning through Personal Narrative

SYDNEY BUTLER
ROY BENTLEY

Pippin Publishing

Copyright © 1997 by Pippin Publishing Corporation
85 Ellesmere Road
Suite 232
Scarborough, Ontario
M1R 4B9

Designed by John Zehethofer
Edited by Pat Hancock
Printed and bound in Canada by Friesens

Canadian Cataloguing in Publication Data

Butler, Sydney James, 1930-
    Lifewriting: learning through personal
    narrative

(The Pippin teacher's library)
Includes bibliographical references.
ISBN 0-88751-042-6

1. Autobiography. 2. English language - Study
and teaching. I. Bentley, Roy, 1931- . II. Title.
III. Series.

CT25.B87 1996   808'.06692   C96-931721-2

ISBN 0-88751-042-6

10   9   8   7   6   5   4   3   2   1

CONTENTS

· · · · · · · · · · · · · · ·

WHAT IS LIFEWRITING?

"Man is essentially a story-telling animal."

A. McIntyre

"We write to heighten our own awareness of life. We write to taste life twice, in the moment and in retrospection."

Anaïs Nin

Lifewriting is the written form of one of our most basic human activities — telling personal stories. Most of our social activity is based on our proclivity to tell each other about our lives. It has been suggested that this kind of social gossip is the human equivalent of the mutual grooming that provides social bonding in ape communities. Instead of picking fleas and nits off each other, we talk about the things that happen to us and our perceptions of the world. Sharing thoughts and experiences in this way enables us to establish our own individuality and to recognize the uniqueness of others.

Lifewriting records this individuality and uniqueness. Encompassing all the various written forms that personal narratives may take, it is an activity open to everyone because we all have stories about our lives to tell. Telling these stories is the very stuff of human communication. Whether oral or written, the articulation of memoirs, anecdotes and reflections on significant people, places and events enables us to discover the meanings and value of the people and events that give shape to life itself.

Our lifewriting project started when we invited elderly people to use writing processes to explore the meanings in their lives. We could have used the term autobiographical writing, but we did not want to create expectations that participants would be required to write a whole book. Lifewriting allowed senior writers the flexibility to compose short personal narratives about their experiences, ideas and feelings about the world. Moreover, as a form of life review, it enabled the writers to see more clearly the themes and values that shaped their lives.

The possibilities for lifewriting in schools became very apparent when we asked our group of seniors meeting at a recreation center to share their stories with a class of 13- and 14-year olds in a neighboring school. The responses of the students to the seniors' stories, and vice versa, convinced us that expressing and sharing life stories was just as important for the youngsters as for their elders.

Since that early experiment we have conducted many lifewriting sessions and courses with many different groups at both the primary and intermediate levels in elementary schools, and with various classes in high schools and colleges. We have even had success in inducing groups of teachers to participate in their own lifewriting workshops. In addition, we have found lifewriting to be successful with adults pursuing basic literacy, with students learning English as a second language, and with people learning to overcome physical disabilities.

When we introduce a group to the processes of lifewriting we emphasize writing as a form of thinking that helps us discover what we think and how we feel. Lifewriting can be the jottings that result from talking not only about past events in our lives, but also about something happening today or that might happen in the future, including our dreams and hopes as well as real possibilities and opportunities. And this kind of exploration need not be bounded by facts; we can also make lifewriting the basis of fiction and poetry.

In short, lifewriting can deal with motivations and reactions to present living, or with possible, probable, or even fantastic futures. Everyone can do it because everyone has lived. And while not many of us are compulsive writers like Anaïs Nin, for example, we can all benefit from the heightened awareness of life that Nin says writing can bring. Through lifewriting, students in particular can transcend the moment of which she speaks to become more aware of the processes by which they learn and the goals of their lifelong learning.

Why Lifewriting in Schools?

But there is a more basic reason for using lifewriting in schools. Lifewriting is central to what Maxine Hairston has called "the new paradigm for teaching writing." In *The Winds of Change*, an analysis of changes in writing programs over the past 20 years, Hairston emphasizes that writing is an act of discovery for both skilled and unskilled writers. In lifewriting, discovery begins with the exploration of the self.

Lifewriting also provides students with strategies for discovering the self. And once students become committed to their own stories, they need to share these stories with other audiences, both in the classroom and at home, and with the world in general.

As well, lifewriting is a recursive process, providing time, opportunity and motivation to expand and revise stories as more information comes to light. It is also a way of learning that includes writing in various forms, with life stories and their accompanying feelings and opinions expressed in expository as well as purely autobiographical modes.

Lifewriting is also very much in accord with our concept of a whole-language classroom. It is real writing, engaging the writer in a serious and committed exploration of experience. It is writing done for oneself, not simply in response to an assigned topic such as Stories about Me, My Opinions about Capital Punishment or the infamous What I Did on My Summer Holidays. It's worth noting, however, that while generations of students returning to school have groaned when confronted with an assignment to tell about their vacation, the Canadian author W.O. Mitchell has written a very entertaining novel from the same beginnings. The difference is that he was telling his story, not a story someone else wanted written.

It is important, then, that teachers be leaders, not dictators, when instructing lifewriting classes, and that we, too, explore our own experiences, feelings and views of the world through lifewriting. Our example is the best way to demonstrate to students how writers take risks, trying out ideas that may or may not succeed. Through our example, we show students the intrinsic messiness of writing — the hesitations and false starts, the crossings out and fresh beginnings that enable both beginners and skilled writers to discover the best form of expression for their ideas.

So, both as models of writers at work and as fellow writers engaged in the same process as the students, teachers of written composition should begin by composing themselves — and the ambiguity here is intentional.

Where in the School?

Lifewriting is such a basic human process that it has its place in any program that uses and values written composition. At first it may seem that lifewriting is the domain of English or language arts teachers because, traditionally, they are assigned to teach the population to write. But, more and more, especially since the Bullock Committee of Enquiry produced its 1975 report, titled *A Language for Life*, writing is viewed as a medium for learning across the entire school curriculum. Accordingly, when students examine human experience in a social studies or guidance class, record perceptions about the environment in science, or respond to the creations of others in art and music, lifewriting can personalize their subject-specific learning. Once they have gained confidence in the power of self-expression, they can use this power to articulate their own learning and to become conscious of their own learning processes.

The Values of Lifewriting

A major strength of lifewriting is its inclusiveness. It shows that everyone has stories to tell, especially if someone is willing to listen, and encourages everyone — young and old alike — to communicate both orally and in writing. As well, because it is autobiographical, lifewriting helps us know both ourselves and others better. It also creates a sense of self-identity and self-worth, and a respect for each individual's uniqueness that promotes social cohesion.

More specifically, lifewriting engages students in the writing process, providing them with both the opportunity and the motivation to improve their writing skills. Over time, it builds confidence in their power to hold the attention of other people, a confidence that extends to report and essay writing too. It also fosters students' interest in revision as they strive to get their stories "right" so that other people will listen to or read about their experiences. In effect, lifewriting transforms all students into authors, and guarantees success for all participants.

All these ideas will be explored in depth in the following chapters, but it is always worthwhile to discuss with students the values of lifewriting right from the start. If they're aware of the benefits, they'll be able to compare their gains to those that other lifewriters have reported in the past, or to students' comments in the first teacher's story that follows.

TEACHER'S STORY: *What Do Students Think about Life-writing?*

EARL MANSFIELD

Earl Mansfield, an experienced social studies teacher and a PhD student in curriculum studies, interviewed 13- and 14-year-old students engaged in a lifewriting unit at the beginning of their first year in a large city high school. Here are some of their comments.

Idea Generation

Several students expressed the view that the lifewriting process helped generate more ideas and alleviate writer's block.

Lola: It gives more ideas for your stories and stuff. It gives you more choices...you're not always stuck on the same things.
Jason: I've got more ideas in my head than I thought.

Shana found that being able to choose her own topics generated what she felt to be better ideas. Renee expressed a similar view.

Shana: I like to pick my own subject. I don't always do as good as I can if I don't pick my own subject.
Renee: It seems like if somebody doesn't tell you what to write, it's a lot easier to write stuff down.

Self-Discovery

Other students found that lifewriting unlocked their memories, permitting them to discover something new about themselves.

Franco: Takes me back a bit.... brings back memories from my past.
Raquel: You're kind of looking back on your situation and you kind of go over what happened. You can see maybe what you could have done different. It kind of opens up into something different...You put more thought into it.

Lynn was a Cantonese speaker having some difficulty with English.

Lynn: It reminds you of all your memories...learn more, more about yourself.

Sandra enjoyed the sense of surprise in discovering new aspects of her "self" as they emerged from her written work. Jason said something similar.

Sandra: You can write things down and you don't know what you're writing about.
Jason: I guess I've seen more things about myself that I didn't see before.

Writing Improvement

Several students felt that the lifewriting process had improved their writing skills. Many attributed an improvement in their writing ability to the focus that the lifewriting process brought to their narratives. Others found that the lifewriting process focused their memories.

Dave: Since I came in, I improved my writing.
Sandra: I've learned how to express my feelings on paper more.
Regan: It's not too hard — it's not too easy. You don't have to think about what you're writing about. You already know what you're writing about. You don't waste a lot of time.
Lindsay: My hardest problem is deciding what you're going to write about. It helps to narrow it down.
Michaela: It helps me, like, figure out...It helps me figure out my thoughts.
Bindi: Expressing what you've done in your life and stuff...I can always remember the details and stuff because you're writing everything.
Giancarlo: It kind of helps me think about stuff I hadn't thought of before...that I wouldn't think of on a normal basis.

Writing Enjoyment

For some students, the lifewriting process made writing more enjoyable or provided motivation.

Marietta: I don't like writing at home. It's not fun...nobody to share it with. But at school I like it because I have more people to share it with.
Elton (a recent refugee from Croatia): This project wakes me up in different ways, so I can do my work.
Alan: The forced writing — it kind of gets your brain going. It helps you think about what to write.

Mike's initial reaction was an unequivocal "I hate writing!" However, he was pleased with the progress he made through the lifewriting process.

Mike: It's made me write a bit...'cause I never usually write. So now I am. I feel good that I'm actually doing some writing.

Ownership of the Writing Process

Still other students appreciated the measure of control the lifewriting process gave them over decision-making and evaluation.

Terri: Because you have freedom to write! You don't have to show it if you don't want to, and people don't make remarks about it.
Roy: You don't have to get it perfect the first time. I think it's a good way to learn how to write.
Leif: Helpful. I like the way you could get your ideas down on paper. There's not much pressure...giving yourself a chance to look back over all your drafts and picking one that's right for you, and then making it right for others. In the process of doing that you get a better chance of getting a good mark.

ESL Language and Writing Development

English was not the first language of about half of the students interviewed. Several students had difficulty responding in English. The most common natal languages other than English were Italian, Cantonese and Japanese.

Stanley, a Japanese speaker, felt that the lifewriting process had improved his vocabulary. Momoko, also a Japanese speaker, expressed the view that writing about personal experience made the writing process easier. For Judy, a Cantonese speaker, the lifewriting process helped her to think in written form, and to include details she would not normally consider when communicating orally. Karmen, a Philippine Canadian who speaks Tagalog, felt that lifewriting enabled her to express feelings she couldn't articulate orally.

Stanley: I've got better words in my sentences.
Momoko: Like, when you get to write about your experiences and that, you have more to write about.

Judy: You need to pay attention to all the details…because you have to write it so that everybody else knows what you know.

Karmen: Like you get to let out your feelings. Sometimes you can't let it out, but you can write it on paper.

Negative Responses

Several students, mainly boys, expressed dissatisfaction with or ambivalence about the lifewriting process. Two expressions of dissatisfaction related to perceived omissions in the lifewriting process. The students remained unaware that these omissions were, in fact, elements of the lifewriting process.

Clive was unaware that students had been asked to bring their own pictures to use as "triggers" during this lifewriting unit.

Clive: I don't know…I'm not interested in it. If he let us look at a picture and write our own story about it, maybe….

Peter felt that using the computer might help him enjoy writing more. He was not aware that using computers would be a part of the process at a later stage.

Peter: I don't really like writing much.

Cherie was unhappy with the segmented nature of the lifewriting process.

Cherie: I don't really like doing it. I'd rather have lots of time on one story rather than just, like, a little bit of time for each story.

Brad felt that lifewriting had not helped his writing skills and had made little difference to him. Significantly, though, despite his negative opinion, he responded positively.

Brad: Well, I liked all of it, but….

· · · · · · · · · · · · · ·

BEGINNING LIFEWRITING

"Writing flourishes where personal expression is valued."
Donald H. Graves

"There are places I remember all my life."
John Lennon and Paul McCartney

Before beginning our enterprise, it is valuable to have a vision of what we want to achieve. We see the students as a group of authors, each committed to expressing his or her own ideas. We see every student as an author engaged in the individual struggle to make meaning out of written words.

Teachers at all levels share this same vision. They all want students, whether young children at the primary level or older children and adolescents, to become competent writers.

We know, as authors and teachers ourselves, that the struggle may not be easy. We use trial-and-error and all sorts of mnemonics to generate ideas. We make plans, drafts and false starts, and we do lots of crossing out and deleting, constantly re-reading our tentative texts to see if the writing on the paper or the images on the computer screen reflect the ideas that seem important to us.

At first our ideas may be jumbled, like a tangled ball of wool. We have to find a loose end to start. As we pull the thread out, it may break, and we have to start somewhere else. We have to make decisions about what comes first. When our ideas are set down on paper, they follow each other in a linear sequence, and we have to check back to see whether the connections between the strings of ideas will be clear and logical to another reader.

In reality, however, the students may not be so dedicated to the task. From their earliest experiences of literature, they have usually encountered texts that are perfect. They have read stories that are correctly formed, spelled, punctuated and printed. They may not appreciate that apparently simple texts in a school reader may be the result of many drafts by the author that usually incorporate suggestions and revisions by others — friends, professional readers, copy editors and proofreaders.

Moreover, in traditional writing programs, they see that the most successful writers are those who can correctly write a required number of words within a set time limit on an assigned topic, with little or no time for research or germination of ideas, major re-writes or feedback from any audience. Within this system, many students will have learned that their best chance of survival lies in writing about simple, obvious ideas using a limited vocabulary, taking no risks, and staying with a familiar, straightforward style to meet the teacher's or the examiner's expectations. In other words, the student learns what sells.

In preparation for introducing lifewriting, it can be helpful to survey the class to see how students perceive the purposes of their writing. The following list of statements can provide a starting point for this kind of discussion. Ask students whether the statements are true or false.

Students write in school:

— To record and learn facts and concepts in each subject.
— To test what they've learned in each subject.
— To test their writing ability.
— To express their own ideas.
— To help express their thoughts about themselves.
— To communicate these ideas and thoughts to others.
— To create their own literary "art."
— As a form of punishment.

The primary purpose of a lifewriting project is to engage writers with their texts, not to record or test facts and concepts. Students need to know that they are being offered an opportunity to write about issues that are important to them, to re-create significant experiences, to comment on the world from their points of view. From the outset, they should be given the following lifewriting guarantees:

— Everyone has stories to tell.

— Everyone can be an author.

— Everyone will get as much help as necessary.

Overcoming Writing Apprehension

Some students, especially those who have been "burned" by past experiences with writing, may need more than guarantees. These students have learned that expressing their own ideas doesn't get them good marks, especially if their work is returned with numerous errors highlighted. They know that these errors are the reason for their discounted scores, and they are afraid to have their writing evaluated. They can't imagine that anyone could possibly enjoy reading what they write and, naturally, they expect to do poorly in a composition class.

When given a test of writing apprehension, these are the students who respond very strongly to statements such as, "I avoid writing," "I'm nervous about writing," "I'm no good at writing," "I never seem to be able to write my ideas clearly," or "My mind seems to go blank when I start to work on a composition." Even at the primary level we find students who assume that every word they write will be inspected to see whether the letters are correctly formed and the spelling is right.

Apprehensive students need to be reassured that the three guarantees mentioned earlier are not simply hollow promises. Fortunately, the teacher of a lifewriting unit can use several techniques for helping them overcome their apprehension and relieve tension in the classroom. Here are two that have worked well for us:

The word bank: Simply listing the words we associate with a topic can function as a technique for generating ideas. The teacher first asks students to look around the room and note all the things they can see. Then she invites them to write down as many of these things as they can during a timed two-minute period. Spelling doesn't count. Afterwards, the teacher can give a "prize" to the student having the most words. Thirty to 40 is not unusual.

Even more important, ask students to compare their lists. This helps them see that everyone has a unique list because everyone perceives the room in an individual way. Recognition can be given for anyone who has listed something that no one else has noticed. The real learning to be drawn from this game is that the act of writing helps everyone become more perceptive. It enables them to record their observations for comparison. And all the students will realize that, for the two minutes of concentrated activity, they have used writing without worrying about it — without being conscious of it as writing *per se*.

The game can be repeated with slightly different prompts:

— Invite students to list all the objects that start with the letter B or the B sound, or all objects that are blue, or round, just as in the traditional game of I Spy.
— Ask them to list everything they can see in a large picture or projected slide.
— Assemble a table full of various objects, covered with a cloth. Remove the cloth for a few seconds, and challenge students to list all the things they remember seeing.
— Invite students to picture a familiar room — a bedroom or family room at home — and list all the objects in that room.

The writing race: This game challenges students to write continuously for five minutes. The aim is to keep the pen or pencil moving, writing whatever ideas come into their heads without worrying about spelling, punctuation, or whether the ideas are sensible. Students may write about anything, following one topic for the full five minutes or switching topics as often as they like.

To begin, the students copy down the sentence: "I don't know what to write about." Assure them that before they reach the end of the sentence, they will already have hundreds of ideas flowing through their minds, and they only have to pick up on one to maintain the flow of writing. The students also need to be reassured that no one is going to read their writing, and they will not be required to read it aloud. It will remain completely private. Afterwards, the teacher can give some form of recognition to the student who has written the most words, or to anyone who is surprised by the ideas that have appeared on the page.

This activity demonstrates the principle that writing is an act of discovery and exploration — that writing does not merely record our thoughts, but is actually an act of thinking in itself. Peter Elbow, in his book *Writing without Teachers,* uses the similar technique of "forced writing" as a means of getting ideas down and overcoming writer's block. In *The Under-achieving School,* John Holt also describes a "writing derby" as a means of overcoming his students' fear of writing.

For students, the most important realization is that they are able to write and think, without worrying about the act of writing itself. For those five minutes, writing became a completely automatic function. They also learn how many words they can write in five minutes. This information can be very reassuring, especially for those who view an essay assignment simply as an overwhelming demand to produce a required number of words. Once they have written 100-150 words in a five-minute "free-write," they will not find the task of generating a 500-word essay as daunting.

A First Experiment in Lifewriting — "Places"

Places provide the settings for our life stories. When we think about where we have lived, loved, played, worked, visited and learned, then we can begin to see the multitude of stories that make up our life history. But at the beginning of a life-writing project, it isn't necessary to discuss the larger issues of life review. For the student in school, the challenge of producing a word bank based on personal experience is enough, although the teacher can help by demonstrating on the chalkboard or overhead projector how his own list expanded to include "places" students might not have considered initially.

At this stage, it is enough to invite students to make a list of places important to them, with the explanation that "place" can mean a house, apartment, cabin, or even a particular room or corner in a particular dwelling. "Place" can also mean a location such as a garden, beach, lake, forest, mountain, road, highway or trail. "Place" may also mean a location where they have spent a lot of their spare time, like a secret hideaway, a treehouse, a special park, or even the local shopping mall. Some may contribute places linked to significant activities, perhaps a ball field or ice-rink, or the seat of a trail-bike or the saddle of a horse.

Give everyone a few minutes to make a list titled Places Important to Me. Encourage them to make as long a list as possible, including every type of place that comes to mind. It is not necessary to time this activity. Simply monitor the lists and end the activity when concentration begins to flag.

There is some value in seeing which students have compiled the longest lists, but the content of the list — and particularly the uniqueness of each person's selection — is more important. Ask the students to compare lists with a partner. Then invite everyone to choose one place on the list to write about and to tell their partners the reason for that choice.

Ownership of the Writing Topic

Enabling students to choose from a list of possible topics is an important principle of lifewriting. The aim is to help them see that they have many possible stories to tell and that if one topic doesn't work, they have others to fall back on. Choice also implies an initial engagement with the topic; students realize that their choices are uniquely theirs. Throughout the lifewriting project, emphasize the students' ownership of the topic, the fact that they know more about this special place than anyone else, and that only they can re-create this place in writing.

Pre-Writing: Idea-Generation

Here's where the results of activities such as creating a word bank and playing the writing race game come into play. Ask students to record their chosen place at the top of a blank piece of paper and draw a small rectangle (about 2 x 3 cm — 1 x $1\frac{1}{2}$ in.) in the middle of the page. Explain that this box represents a picture of the place they're about to describe, and ask them to concentrate on it. Some may wish to sketch in a few details, but a blank box works just as well.

Now the brainstorming can begin. Ask them to list everything they "see" in the picture. As words begin to flow on to paper, invite students to make an imaginative transformation to think about the sounds they can hear in the picture, the smells and tastes they associate with it, and the textures — smooth or grainy surfaces, soft or rough materials — they can feel when they stretch out a hand into the picture. Next they add the names of the living things in their picture — specific plants, flowers, trees, birds, animals or pets. Then they list the people associated with the picture, and finally the moods or feelings they recall when they think about this place. To provide closure to this pre-writing activity, students might compose a title or headline for their story.

Telling Writing

At this point, students will have generated a mass of unsorted and undifferentiated ideas. Before they attempt to transform this into sequential prose, it's best if they have an opportunity to talk to their partners again, telling them more about their place, what they remembered about it during the listing activity, and especially why it is important to them. The oral activity should end with the students composing one sentence on the paper to introduce the place. On their sheets, they should also mark the words that represent the most important ideas.

We have detailed these idea-generating techniques in the pre-writing stage because they set a pattern for further experiments in lifewriting. In this first lesson, the opportunity to talk over ideas with a partner has been limited to specific points in the composing process. Nevertheless, these short episodes of talking are very important for establishing trust between writer and reader. This trust is the foundation of the more extensive conferences and peer-response activities that are so essential to the collaborative approach to the teaching of writing discussed in the chapter titled "Collaboration in the Lifewriting Class."

First Draft Lifewriting — "An Important Place"

After these pre-writing activities, students should be ready to begin their first draft. In the interests of creating a supportive and reassuring atmosphere, the teacher must re-affirm that this first draft is part of the experiment to find out whether the place is worth writing about. It must be seen as a beginning. Students will not be expected to write everything they know about the place. Some, indeed, may find out that the place they chose is the wrong place, and they are free to switch to another topic at any time.

Establish a time limit of 10 minutes for this first draft. Urge students to write as continuously as possible, but remind them that they can refer to their word lists and the picture if they need to think of new ideas. The teacher also needs to make it clear that she, too, will be participating in this activity as a writer. In fact, many teachers have remarked that they enjoy teaching the lifewriting unit because it gives them a chance to be writers themselves. For students, it is a salutary lesson to realize that, while they are writing, the teacher is too. At first, they may look up occasionally to check that she is, and will be reassured to realize that this really is an activity for all writers, not merely another school exercise.

The teacher can also insist upon silence because everyone, herself included, needs to be in touch with the ideas flowing from mind to pen to paper. Students will also be comforted to know that they are not expected to finish their story in this session. This is a first draft, and there will be opportunities to add to it and change it during the revision stage.

After the silent writing session, some students will want to keep their work private; others will want to share their stories with their partners. The more confident ones may even want to read their pieces to the entire class. Try to accommodate these individual differences because, ultimately, all students need to discover which techniques work best for them.

The closure of this writing episode is the need to treat both the list of words and the first draft as part of a "work-in-progress," writing drafts that must be preserved because they may contain valuable ideas for further revision and publication. At this point, it is necessary for the teacher to make sure the drafts don't get lost in the hurly-burly of school notes and assignments. Many schools have already instituted a policy of maintaining individual writing portfolios (see the chapter titled "Evaluating Lifewriting") for this purpose, but teachers can improvise by providing manila folders or large envelopes in which students can safeguard their writing.

JOHN PICONE

Envisioning my fifth-period English class — a combination of students at two distinct levels of ability — usually conjures up images of bleeding wrists. And some days were like that. But not that Friday when I invited the students to bring a photograph to class. Indeed, this particular Friday remains indelibly impressed upon my memory as one of the most intense and energetic, most *real* writing moments I have ever known as an English teacher of many years' experience.

Now, a few facts are germane to this memory of mine. It's Friday afternoon and a spectacularly sunny day outside our well-windowed third-floor classroom. It's the last period of the day — and of the week. Further, we have been told that the third-floor classes will be helping to move furniture to the newly renovated wing of the school to which we will migrate the following Tuesday. In other words, that class was an interrupted last period of a sunny Friday afternoon before a long weekend. It was also the class during which I said, "Get together with one of your buddies and tell each other about your picture. What's going on in the picture? What happened before? Or after? Why is it important to you?"

The chatter was unquenchable! Young people who had said practically nothing all semester were bursting at the seams to tell their stories.

"Okay. Now be by yourself for a few minutes. Take a sheet of loose-leaf paper and draw a small square in the middle of the page. Now, imagine that's your picture. You can even sketch it, if you like. Surround it with words and phrases that describe it."

Some further prompts were needed here.

"You remember our discussion about setting and imagery? Okay, let's get some sights and sounds and tastes and smells and texture. What did people say? How did you feel at the time? Jot down as much as you can. Don't stop writing."

An unprecedented quiet descended on the room at this point. Only the whisper of the pens and pencils on the paper could be heard.

I then asked the students to put away the page they had just been writing on, take the photograph in their non-writing hand, and hold it before them.

"Now, I'd like you to have an audience in mind as you write. It can be anyone, someone real who knows you and is important to you, but someone who knows nothing about this special picture. Perhaps you would like to write to me. Whoever it is, keep that person in mind all the while, and tell him or her all about your picture."

I also indicated that this was like a rough draft, a work in progress. It didn't have to be perfect. There would be ample opportunity to revise it later if they wanted to.

We finally had to bring things to a close and move the chairs and desks from our room. For more than 20 minutes, no one had stopped writing. I was amazed. What I had witnessed was unlike anything I had ever seen before in my — or anyone else's — English classroom.

While I have come to understand the importance of what James Moffett calls "the will behind the mind," I had never really thought it could be brought to life in a secondary English class with this kind of vitality.

Lifewriting is clearly a great "teacher" to students and teachers of writing. Certainly it was eloquent testimony to something I've come to believe about all growth in language, whether written or oral: it has to matter. "Vital impressions and convictions," as John Dewey calls it. And it revealed to me that the life story of any young person is a wonderfully rich and exciting topic to write about.

Perhaps more important is what lifewriting teaches the young writer. For students in 4G/B, it makes the unequivocal point that they can write! The sheer volume of their production overwhelmed many of them.

"I wrote more in this class," said John, "than I did in English all last year!"

But the experience also tells young people that their lives are interesting, special, unique and well worth telling about. Maybe that's the most important lesson.

. . . .

DEVELOPING LIFEWRITING
UNITS AND PROGRAMS

"Writing, like life itself, is a voyage of discovery."

Henry Miller

"For me the initial delight is in the surprise of remembering something I didn't know I knew."

Robert Frost

This chapter does two things: it suggests a number of ways to get a class started in lifewriting, and it follows through with basic structures for a lifewriting unit or program.

Keys to Unlocking Memories and Ideas

The "Places" activity described in detail in the previous chapter is a powerful tool for overcoming apprehension, getting people interested, and persuading them to put pen to paper. We have used it successfully with groups ranging in age from seven to 70, getting everyone involved from the outset in telling and writing their own stories and expressing their own ideas and opinions. The support and encouragement flowing from the collaborative processes we'll describe in the following chapter are just as important for sustaining the drive towards revision and publication.

But it's not necessary, or even desirable, for every class session to follow the same lock-step, teacher-directed routine. Instead, once students have overcome the first hurdle on the path to becoming authors, it's unlikely that all of them will proceed at the same rate. For some, alternative routes to success may be needed when the chosen starter activity doesn't seem to work.

The following ideas — keys to unlocking memories — are more than simply starters. They can also generate a series of experiments in which the participants write in order to find out whether they have something to write about. In most cases, the keys will help them find something in their experience that grabs them.

Keys to Unlocking Memories

Places
Danger
Snapshots
Show and Tell
Memorable Moments
Letters I Should Have Written
Letters to Famous People
Journeys
Arrivals and Departures
Turning Points
Flowers
Changes
And I Never Told Anyone
Holidays and Festivals
Gangs
Jobs
Dances
Concerts
Heroes
Smoking and Drinking
Favorite Toys
Swings and Roundabouts
Bikes, Cars and Motorbikes
Crimes and Misdemeanors
Clothes
The Time of My Life

Some of the ideas will work for most students, and most of them will work for some students. The hope is that every student will be able to find something that works and quite possibly students themselves will suggest other topics that can be added to the list.

But a word of caution is in order. It is important to present the list, not as teacher-assigned topics, but as ideas that have worked as triggers for others. Any of the topics can serve as a subject for class discussion or group brainstorming. The aim is for each student to make the topic personal by thinking of an experience that connects in some way to the common topic. It is not important to stick zealously to the topic. Instead, each topic is designed to act as a key to help individuals generate unique, personal ideas and thoughts.

The teacher can expand the topics by posing questions that stimulate open-ended thinking. Here's a sampling of the kinds of questions that might be used with some of the topics:

Places
What places are important in our lives — places where we live, play, work, visit, travel, hang out?

The Time of My Life
What were (are) the best of times, the worst of times?

Danger
What were the occasions when life or safety was threatened — accidents, getting lost, fire, drowning, fights, threats (real or imagined), fears?

Firsts
What are the "firsts" we remember — first memories, first toys, first bike, first camping trip, first dentist, first time away from home, first flight, first train ride, first day at school, first friend, first enemy, first award, first pet, first success?

Snapshots
What snapshot or picture of something important in our life — an event, trip, person — can we show and talk about to a small group?

Letters I Should Have Written
To whom do we owe apologies or explanations?

Letters to Famous People
Who are our public heroes, or villains? What could we say to them?

Some teachers may prefer to use more general themes to open up discussion and writing. The following recurring themes are drawn from both our experience and research:

Themes of Adolescence

Jobs
Love

Friendships
Achievements
Disappointments
Independence
Rebellion
Dreams
Self-awareness
Relationship With Parents
Authority
Character Flaws
Law and Order
Embarrassments
Regrets
Heroes
Wishes

Themes like these offer students an opportunity to express their opinions in an expository mode if they wish to do so, rather than in the narrative mode more common to lifewriting. Students who want to keep their experiences private benefit from the safety of third-person distancing.

Nevertheless, all students should be encouraged to embody within their texts short life stories as examples and illustrations of the ideas they wish to convey. Concrete examples derived directly from their life experiences will serve them well by giving their abstract ideas a convincing, factual grounding.

For example, in a senior high school scholarship essay examination, students were asked to state their opinions about the benefits of amateur sports. One student rambled on for two pages, discussing in abstract terms health, fitness, involvement and responsibility. Had she finished at that point her essay might well have been judged a failure. But, just as she seemed to run out of vague abstractions, she suddenly switched to writing about her own interest in equestrian sports. Immediately, her writing was revived as she described her own experiences with horses. The vague abstractions became concrete and convincing as she drew real lessons from her own life, and they satisfied well the demands of the essay assignment.

This example reminds us of the value of incorporating narratives of personal experience to support arguments in expository writing. As Harold Rosen suggests in *Stories and Their Meanings*, "Inside every non-narrative kind of discourse there stalk the ghosts of narrative." The hope is that, like the list of more specific keys to memory, these themes may encourage some students to express their views about issues that are central to their adolescent lives.

Questions for Unlocking Memories and Ideas

Questioning is one of the most effective ways of unlocking memories and generating ideas. The questions may come from oneself, working independently, or from others in set collaborative exercises. Self-questioning works well for the reflective person engaged in interpreting and crafting incidents and facts that have already come to mind or are included in rough notes or first drafts. Questioning by others is immensely stimulating and highly productive in eliciting information that may even surprise the writer. But questioning is more than simply a procedure for prompting answers or provoking memories. When applied to oneself, it is also a way of thinking.

Although even casual and random questions, if posed seriously, seem to work well in drawing ideas and emotions to the surface, the initial questions can be made more potent if follow-up questions are asked. In other words, rather than being satisfied with the factual answer to a "what" question such as, "What is your earliest memory?" the questioner probes further. "Why do you remember this particular event?" "Did it have a special effect that makes it stand out?" "Was this unusual?" "How do you feel about it now?" "How did you feel about it at the time?" The aim is not just to revisit the incident, but to open doors to more memories and many more details.

A more sophisticated approach to intensive exploration is to use various levels of questions, ranging from those that elicit mostly factual answers through to those that require analysis or synthesis of the experiences. The following list indicates the aim of different levels of questioning and provides some sample question starters:

Recall — the Facts
What do you remember?

Where and when did it happen?

Understanding — The Meaning of the Facts
What was happening here?
Why was it important for you?

Probes — Generalizations about the Facts
How did this affect...?
How does this compare to...?

Analysis — The Reasons behind the Facts
Why do you think this happened?
What effect did this have?

Reconstruction — Ways to Change the Facts
How would you change...?
What might you have done differently?
Would this have happened differently in another time or place?

Evaluation — Assessment of the Incident
What is your attitude to the happening (occasion,people) now?
Have there been any continuing or long-term effects?
Looking back, what would you have done differently?

Exploring a topic or theme using appropriate levels of questioning can stimulate powerful responses in all group members, often resulting in prolonged and detailed debate. Time spent in this way should not be viewed as time away from writing, but as a rehearsal for later work at a greater level of complexity.

Using questions to explore various aspects of a topic or theme also unlocks memories and stimulates ideas. One method, most effective when dealing with a remembered incident, involves the writer or group members in developing questions that focus, when appropriate, on each of the following aspects of the incident:

— The place.
— The people.
— The setting.
— The plot (What was going on?)
— The "times" (When did this happen?)

A more cinematographic approach uses questions designed to direct attention closer and closer to the incident, much as a camera zooms in on its subject. For example, questions can help a writer capture the feeling of a beach scene, bringing to mind the feel of the grains of sand, the sound of the waves, or the bubbles in a line of foam. The reverse — zooming out — can also be effective. The right questions can help place an incident in a broader context, in which it is viewed as a microcosm representative of a larger pattern. Both methods, when allied with various levels of questioning, can be specific workshop writing exercises. Beware, though, of providing too much stimulation. The aim is not to toy superficially with many possibilities, but to discover one or two ideas that will engage a person enough that she or he wants to explore, discuss and write.

The Lifewriting Unit and Program

Any of the preceding strategies can be used successfully for the occasional writing assignment and in any general writing program. In particular, the pre-writing and drafting approaches ease the way into all forms of composition. So, before introducing lifewriting, a teacher can try out these approaches in her current writing program to see if she feels comfortable with them and if they work with her students.

Two other options are to offer a self-contained two- or three-week lifewriting unit or to substitute a lifewriting program for regular writing activities for one term only. Of course, nothing prevents a teacher from focusing on autobiographical writing for the entire year, incorporating instruction to meet specific needs in, for example, expository or critical writing. Because this last approach is probably impractical for most teachers, however, we shall deal only with the unit and the term programs.

UNIT OUTLINE

The unit is based on a three-stage approach involving pre-writing, writing and post-writing. For ease of description, the sample unit that follows is based on three weeks, but it can be compressed or expanded to fit class scheduling and students' needs and interests.

Week 1: Pre-Writing

Explain the focus and approaches of the lifewriting unit, stressing that:

— Everyone has something to write about.
— There is no pressure to reveal anything the student doesn't want to reveal.
— Collaborative stimulation and help are always available.
— There'll be no emphasis on "correctness" until the editing stage.

Activities:

— Teacher leads discussion of appropriate items from the list of keys to unlocking memories.
— Teacher uses questions to focus reminiscences.
— Participants choose one idea and develop a related word cache, idea-clustering chart, list of incidents or drawings.
— If the initial idea is unproductive, the student is encouraged to try another topic.

The products expected at the end of this phase include lists, jottings, notes, diagrams, fragments and rough drafts from which possibilities for more sustained writing will come. The teacher might want to help proceedings along by reading a few of his own beginnings or short selections by published authors and poets, or by inviting some students to share excerpts from their work-in-progress with the class.

Week 2: Writing

Explain that students may work alone, with a peer, or in groups. The aim is to get a first draft on paper. Checking on grammar, spelling or punctuation can come later.

Activities:

— Working in pairs, students interview each other about the ideas they are toying with and what they are going to focus on in the next draft.
— Students write (or tell, dictate or tape-record) their stories, trying them out as necessary on their partners.

— Where appropriate, students might be encouraged to seek more information or to test their ideas with friends or relatives.

The products expected at the end of this week need not be long or completely shaped. They could take the form of a letter, a poem, a journal entry, an incident, an anecdote, a portrait, or a fragment from a possible larger work.

Week 3: Post-Writing

Explain that the goal is to complete a final copy to be included in the student's portfolio. To this end, the resources of the group should be used to get audience reactions. Group assistance is also available for checking, editing and polishing.

Activities:

— Groups of four or five share their writing, with participants responding, commenting, helping (with words, spelling, grammar, etc.) and offering suggestions for follow-up and "publication."
— Students rewrite or polish final copies, using peers or the teacher as resources.
— Volunteers share their work with the whole class.
— "Publication" possibilities (on tape, in a class book, in a computer file, etc.) are explored.

The product here should be a piece of writing that students are reasonably happy with because of audience response, feel they have an investment in (and may even want to develop further), and know will meet routine standards of presentation and "correctness."

PROGRAM OUTLINE

The pattern of pre-writing, writing and post-writing is also basic to the structure of the term-long program. The mode we find most productive consists of a series of units similar to the one just described. The intent is to have students producing a number of shorter pieces destined for their portfolios, developing facility in writing along the way and, perhaps, settling on an idea, topic or essay that will lead to the longer, sustained work that comes at the end of the program.

Assuming that the unit outline just presented is the introduction, the following stages would complete the outline for the entire term:

Writing from Memories

Pre-Writing
Keys to unlocking memories — places, people, events.
Keys to unlocking writing — listing, interviewing, drawing.

Writing
An autobiographical vignette, episode, chapter, introduction, etc.

Post-Writing
Sharing, correcting, rewriting.

Writing from Stimuli

Pre-Writing
Show-and tell — sharing objects, photographs, letters, handicrafts, mementos, badges, trophies, souvenirs, etc.

Writing
Writing in various modes — interviews, dialogue, verse, stories, expositions, instructions, etc.

Post-Writing
Collect all drafts in the portfolio. One or two might be selected for further revision or adaptation to a particular format such as a poem or film script.

Discovering the Patterns

Pre-Writing
Share how incidents in life connect.
Discuss the plots of movies, TV dramas or series, books, etc. to discover how plots are shaped.

Writing
Develop a longer, sustained piece of writing (perhaps a chapter from a life story; e.g., My Brilliant Career) that is a continuation of something already explored or begun, or that could serve as the start of a new project.

Post-Writing
Sharing writing with group members and other groups while preparing for class presentation or "publication."

The conclusion of the program should concentrate on shaping the material for an audience. Although lifewriting may be intensely personal, it is not necessarily private. The longer work, unless it is not meant for sharing, should be written with presentation in mind. This ensures that correcting, editing and polishing are taken seriously, a sign of respect for the eventual "audience" and because what is worth saying is worth saying well. The presentation is the product of a lot of hard work by a writer who is personally engaged in the project, not merely an attempt to get a passing grade. The final unit, following our basic format, might look something like this:

Final Unit

Pre-Writing
Discussion of what an audience expects from a story, book, TV program, speech, etc.
Teacher-directed lesson on various presentation strategies — catchy beginnings, clinching endings, etc.
Teacher-directed lesson on possible presentation formats — computer-printout, overheads, tape recordings, public readings, etc.
Listing of criteria that might be expected of each group member's work.

Writing
Final copy production with the preceding criteria in mind and with conferences with the teacher as necessary.

Post-Writing
"Publication" in some form — class readings, individual, group or class books, computer bulletin board postings, tape-recordings, school showcase, joint-class presentations, festival of writing, author celebrations, etc.

These basic models for a unit or for a complete program are, of course, suggestions only. They are based on structures that we have found work well, but they should be supplemented by the ideas and material we'll discuss in the following chapter on collaboration and in the chapter titled "Evaluating Lifewriting."

Occasionally, a planned unit or program may begin to disintegrate if some students, entranced by the personal rewards offered by lifewriting, take hold of their own ideas and explore in different directions. If this happens, it's a cause for rejoicing, because the aim of lifewriting is not to slavishly follow a predetermined plan, but to get students writing, and writing well, and to encourage them to take control of their writing.

TEACHER'S STORY: *Lifewriting with 16-Year-Olds*

ANTONIA ZANNIS

Lifewriting is currently playing an integral role in our secondary IV English language arts classes at Villa Maria High School in Montréal, Québec. We used the occasion of the 125th anniversary of Canada and the 350th anniversary of the founding of Montréal to inspire our students to discover their identities within the context of their lives both as Montrealers and Canadians. They are looking to themselves as individuals, speaking with family members about their Canadian heritage and searching for specific information about the first members of their families to arrive in Canada.

Students explored their identities and wrote narratives about their Canadian cultural heritage. In groups, they presented this information in skits, sharing their multicultural identities with each other.

The theme of identity was explored in Canadian literature, especially in *The Apprenticeship of Duddy Kravitz, Two Solitudes* and other novels, short stories, poems, and magazine and newspaper articles. We are also using material written by budding Canadian authors — the students themselves! The students maintained portfolios in which they entered material inspired by class activities, personal readings, individual viewing of films and personal writing.

The final assignment in this unit is a short story that will focus on their identity — a culmination of all the work they have done throughout the term. The students seem to be enjoying this activity. They believe that they have learned a great deal about themselves, their families and other members of the community. Their journey of discovery can be tracked in their portfolios, and both students and teachers alike find this journey fascinating.

. . . .

COLLABORATION

IN LIFEWRITING

"Writing floats on a sea of talk."

Andrew Wilkinson

"Writing has got to be an act of discovery...I write to find out what I'm thinking about."

Edward Albee

A glimpse into a classroom that reflects modern approaches to teaching written composition would show students working together. We might see two students reading and commenting on each other's texts, a group holding a buzz session to come up with or clarify ideas, or a couple composing jointly on a classroom computer. While individual students may be trying out various starter ideas or polishing a draft for editing and publication, the initial energy and extended motivation is provided by students, or students and teacher, working together.

These collaborative and cooperative activities push students to get involved, to take an active role in creating and composing, and eventually to enthusiastically take ownership of their own piece of storytelling.

Today's trends toward student involvement are soundly based on research. Many studies indicate that writing improves when teachers take a process or environmental approach, such as that followed in a writer's workshop format. In a workshop setting, students have a clear sense of purpose for their writing, use collaborative learning to develop their individual skills, and have a teacher available as facilitator, consultant, co-editor and participant in the writing activities. The values of this kind of collaborative approach, summarized here, are worth discussing with any class about to embark on a lifewriting unit or program.

— Collaboration helps get students involved.
— Collaboration opens the creativity floodgates.
— Collaboration develops an awareness of the audience.
— Collaboration encourages revision and editing.
— Collaboration makes the effort of writing worthwhile.

What Sorts of Collaboration?

It is quite easy to get a class started on collaboration. However, the teacher must be aware that a workshop is a place to work — and to work together. It's not a place for lecturing. She has enough other work to do. She has to decide on the physical layout of the classroom, set up an agenda and prepare a schedule, establish procedures for getting things done, and work with the students to identify the goals of the writing project.

It's also important for the workshop to occur on a regular basis, follow a more-or-less fixed pattern, and present a standard set of activities from which students can choose. These routines get students talking and writing, and help keep them talking and writing.

The simplest way to start is to give the class an initial briefing covering the purpose, structure, methods and schedule. At this stage, too much direction or instruction can be counter-productive. The goal is to get students working together as soon as possible, preferably without direct teacher involvement. Later, if necessary, the teacher can assume advising and counseling roles to keep things rolling. Usually, working in groups of three or four helps overcome any initial reluctance or reticence. Partnerships work well with more mature students who are eager to get started. However, the following stages and corresponding sample activities suggest various ways of working together.

Beyond the introductory briefing, lifewriting workshops proceed through five stages. The first stage, while not formally recognized, is a key element in getting students really involved. It is the getting-ready-to-roll stage, when participants typically try to identify what they are supposed to be doing, what the teacher wants, and to what extent they are going to invest in the activity. They ask questions, seek clarification, elaborate on what they think is expected of them and review proposed tasks and procedures before actually beginning any activity. If all goes well, this clarifying, coordinating, and consensus-testing will continue.

A slow start is to be expected with groups new to lifewriting, but eventually there'll be a great deal of group discussion. Not surprisingly, one or two leaders will emerge, and perhaps a cynic or someone along for a free ride. There'll be frequent requests that the teacher repeat certain instructions and directions, and occasional side-checks with other groups.

During this stage, the teacher is most effective if she holds off involving herself in the groups until after students have had a chance to get started and identify what they need to know. They need time on their own to develop a view of the group as a cohesive and self-contained entity. To help members see the group in this way, the emphasis should be on collaboration between the teacher and the entire group, with individual student-teacher work kept to a minimum.

Here are some activities that can be used to engage the group and promote collaboration:

— Written peer responses to each other's activities.
— Group revision of a sample piece of first-draft writing.
— Writing an introduction for a group anthology.
— Writing a group composition on a shared topic.
— Acting as an editorial board to select stories submitted.

The next four stages of the lifewriting workshop foster further collaboration. The pre-writing phase offers many opportunities to work together. The teacher and students collaborate when identifying topics, trying out various idea-generating techniques and exploring beginnings. Group members work together brainstorming for ideas, identifying promising leads, developing a responsive ear, picking up suggestions, and trying out possibilities. Partners can help each other by acting in turn as audience or author, listening and reacting to each other's trial starts and rough compositions.

During the writing stage, more formal collaborative processes emerge. An awareness of audience reaction grows in the writers, and they begin to hear their own voice too. Audience members — listeners — also benefit by hearing different examples of writing and by gaining insights into what works well with the group. So, collaboration moves beyond the initial search for ideas or joint composition to a shared responsibility for the effectiveness of the writing.

The revision stage must not be seen solely as an editing or error-hunting exercise, but as a time to look again, so to speak. Although group collaboration facilitates revision, partnerships can be more effective, providing the two writers with dress-rehearsal opportunities before works are presented to the entire group and chances to try out alternatives or improved versions with several different partners.

Student-teacher conferences are not recommended at this stage either, since the aim is to encourage students to come up with their own answers and suggestions. The students learn from each other as the whole group, or one member, assumes the role of editor, working with the writer on such things as cutting, adding, checking grammar and spelling, and deciding on effective titles. However, while visiting groups and individuals, the teacher may identify issues that can be presented briefly to the whole class as a sort of status report, but not as a prescriptive lesson.

The final stage — sharing — involves the group in appreciating, reacting and selecting. And just as working in pairs eases students into this stage, sharing within the group can be preliminary to sharing with the teacher, the entire class, or the wider audience reached through such activities as publishing in a school newspaper or reading at a school function.

At every stage, then, collaboration is an integral part of lifewriting activities directed toward encouraging students to produce a finished piece of writing. The group has done its work when this goal has been met. But even then, it's a good idea to keep groups together for a debriefing session when students try to identify what they have learned about the writing process, working collaboratively, and which learning processes work best for them. These sessions can also provide the teacher with insights into ways of making collaboration more effective and efficient. These insights, together with additional writing tips the teacher decides would be helpful after listening to the students' comments, can be passed on in mini-lessons designed to assist groups and partners in the future.

Once groups have had some experience with collaboration, a formal briefing on the process itself may be a more appropriate and productive way to begin other lifewriting units.

Instead of getting group work under way as quickly as possible, as we suggested earlier, the teacher might invite students to explore in more detail topics such as:

— Why collaboration works.
— How we learn from each other.
— The roles we play in groupwork.
— The purposes of brainstorming.
— Questions that stimulate ideas.
— How to learn from each other.

From briefing through to debriefing, it is the leadership style of the teacher that influences the way collaboration moves forward in the classroom. We have found the most effective starting image is that of the teacher as a writing coach. As the following diagram shows, the teacher-coach spends some time organizing and developing activities, but also works with groups and individuals to reduce apprehension and encourage personal engagement.

Understand the principles of lifewriting

Establish writing environment

Develop repertoire of strategies

Reduce apprehension

Encourage exploration and discovery

Memory Keys
Themes   Plans

Promote engagement

Collaboration

Model writing processes

Conferences

We've already indicated how helpful talking to others is when searching for ideas, exploring possible writing topics and story directions, and preparing writing for publication in some form. Donald Murray, one of the pioneers of research into writing processes and a teacher and a writer himself, makes a similar point when he says in *All Writing Is Autobiography*, "Sometimes the writer not only talks to himself or herself, but to others — collaborators, editors, teachers, friends — working out the idea for a piece of writing in oral language with someone else who can enter into the process of discovery with the writer."

We've found that this kind of "telling" writing, when the writer talks about an idea still in the germination stage, is vital. The reciprocal of this process is equally important. The "conference," through questions and suggestions, helps writers shape, clarify, extend and elaborate on their ideas. To help writers in this way, teachers and group members can use questions such as the following in any conference setting:

— What is the main focus of the story?
— Does the beginning of the story grab you?
— Does the story need more detail or information?
— Is information clearly presented?
— Does the story have a good ending?
— Does it end in the right place?

Vincent Wixon and Pat Stone formalized this process at the secondary school level by developing a "talk-write" technique based on the ideas of Robert Zoellner, who developed a behavioral pedagogy for composition. Wixon and Stone's method makes writing a public affair by encouraging students to work in a partnership, with the writer using a felt pen to make a first draft on a large sheet of butcher paper. Meanwhile the "encouraging half" of the team reads, comments and questions the writer while the writing takes shape in full view. While this approach is still valid, the computer screen can provide a less tedious and more convenient public forum for an "encourager" to question the text during the drafting process.

No matter what form the conference takes, it is a powerful engine that drives the writing process. Conferences achieve a number of purposes, as follows:

— Expand the writer's ideas.
— Help writers feel good about their ideas.
— Clarify what the writer has written.
— Provide a sympathetic audience.
— Give the writer a sense of purpose.
— Help the writer to reflect.
— Enable the writer to feel ownership of the writing.
— Empower the writer to persevere.

TEACHER'S STORY: *Building a Community of Memories*

CAROLLYNE SINCLAIRE

It's silent reading time. At last all the "riots" are quelled and we are quiet. The students are spread out on carpets, under desks, and stuffed into corners of the classroom. I am seated near the window, bathing in the sunlight that streams in, almost purring with the satisfaction of a good book.

"Ms. Sinclaire!" Eric Bradbury rushes up to me, clutching a book of poems we wrote last year about significant events in our lives at the time — embarrassing moments, getting caught, first-time experiences, weird food we've eaten, and so on.

"Look Ms. Sinclaire, look!" he blurts out, attempting to whisper, but bellowing instead. "Look at this! It's so cool. This poem — Alex wrote it. Last year."

"Yeah, it is..." I am interrupted before I can continue.

"That was when we were playing softball. Just like we are now. See?" He waits for my nod after pointing out that part in the poem.

"And look," he continues. "Alex — he was afraid of doing bad at baseball then. See? And you know what? Alex is the best on the team now. He never strikes out."

I nod, thinking that both Alex and Eric have learned a lot.

Eric is stunned at his friend's progress in achieving his desires and overcoming his fears. Writing about our lives has made that obvious benchmark of growth visible. Eric is learning that we can change. A fear his friend once had, a legitimate fear, has been overcome.

I could not have set up a better lesson to teach these things than this one serendipitous moment in the classroom. Eric's words remind me of the value of writing and performing our works and taking the time to read our own work and reflect on it later, and to visit and revisit the words in the class book.

Together, as a class, we have built a bank of community memories that link us together and to the past. The memories are further clarified by the "photo album" of the vital moments of our lives, our stories and poems compiled in books to read and share.

We think of children as having little history — smaller files of memory and recollection. Yet, a year in the life of a child provides many more first-time thrills and experiences than does a single year for most of us adults. Re-reading stories about their past experiences and the way they perceived them and themselves at the time gives young readers the opportunity to be in awe of their own growth, maturity and expanding abilities.

After our morning sharing discussions in my classroom, I write with the students. I share my work with them when they share. I try to capture the words that trigger the essence of our conversations. I know the language I use is authentic because my students have given me some feedback. At first, their reaction was one of incredulity; then some became critical and tried to determine the accuracy of my statements.

After one such reading, Eric said, "Ms. Sinclaire, the way you write it, it's true. It's just that it's almost more than true because you got right to the important stuff."

I look around and there is a hush in the classroom. We are all quiet, absorbed in our thoughts and in our writing. The students and I are engaged in "becoming," in shaping ourselves. In writing and reading our work, we teachers bring to a halt the action all around us in order to hear and respond to the call that led us into teaching.

PRACTICAL APPROACHES

IN THE CLASSROOM

"I know my life as an episodic narrative.... In story after story I am protagonist and antagonist, participant and spectator."

Carl Leggo

"How do I know what I think until I see what I say?"

E. M. Forster

Writing is hard work. For many students, its difficulty precludes making anything more than a cursory effort. This is why it's so important to get students interested in writing; if they're interested enough, they'll invest time and energy in it. The aim is to place ownership and primary responsibility in their hands, with the teacher expecting best efforts from all of them, regardless of arbitrary or predetermined ability levels. The teacher can then concentrate on structuring writing experiences geared for success.

This strategy keeps the focus on the value of personal experience as a starting point for writing, and on providing enough in-class time for peer group discussion, analysis, criticism and experimentation. The approach moves away from the view of the teacher as the sole evaluator of both works-in-progress and finished pieces. Her role becomes that of facilitator within a community of writers who value writing, with engagement being at least as important an indicator of capability as grades.

Initial Approaches

We follow three approaches to get students involved.

For example, after preparing the class physically and mentally to concentrate, the teacher might lead students through a series of "recall" exercises, using questions such as the following:

The Present
What were you thinking of five minutes ago?
What did you do yesterday evening?
What did you do last weekend?

The Past
What is your most vivid memory of school last year?
What three things do you remember from the time before you started school?
What was the best holiday you ever had?

The Process
What things are you good at remembering?
How good is your visual memory? Could you make yourself see a snapshot or a video clip of your day today?
How good is your sensory memory? Can you recall the taste, smell, feel or sound of some experience from the weekend?
What helps you remember?
Do you realize that you are creating memories now? If you were asked in 10 minutes to talk about what you are doing now, you would be re-creating an experience.

Questions like these, along with other introductory activities that can be carried out with the whole class — from studying the lifelines in the palm of one's hand to pondering whether or not one's astrological sign is accurate in its description — are important because they enable the teacher to present these initial explorations as serious thought-provoking exercises.

USING GROUP REINFORCEMENT

Again, to launch the lifewriting program the teacher might supply groups with pictures of "strangers" taken from magazines and invite each group to discuss questions such as, Which name would you give this person? Why? What can you imagine about this person's home, family, feelings, future?

What stories could you make up about this person in the picture?

These discussions distance comments on life and living from personal experiences that some students may not be comfortable sharing with others. Once the safety of discussing in a group is assured, encourage students to bring in photographs of their own choosing — of themselves when younger, with their pets, at sports, on holiday, with their family. This activity works best with small groups of three or four.

For more directed questioning, pairing students with a trusted partner is most effective. The "reporter's biography" is an approach to paired questioning that we have used successfully. This technique involves one student in playing the role of reporter while the other is the interview subject. Under the heading (Student's Name) — A Brief Biography, the reporter fills two pages with the interview subject's life data (e.g., where and when born, where grew up, special interests and talents, likes and dislikes, family, friends, pets, plans and hopes for the future). The students then reverse roles and repeat the process.

TAPPING OUTSIDE SUPPORT

Lifewriting can get an infusion of energy if parents, grandparents or relatives are willing to tell students stories about their childhoods or some personal adventures or exploits. If parents are interested, the teacher can provide a list of "trigger" materials or ideas to facilitate discussion of things like family albums, diaries, a family tree, memorabilia or souvenirs, or familiar family tales. Keeping in mind that it is the process of lifewriting and the student's engagement in this process that are important, students can be encouraged to conduct reporter biography interviews with willing relatives or friends. They might even choose to invent biographies for people they meet on the bus, in the library or at a part-time job. Imagined interviews with characters from television shows or the actors behind these roles are another possibility, especially in a group setting, because they offer a chance to compare individual students' reports on the same subject.

From time to time, the teacher may decide to introduce strategies designed to stimulate more detailed reminiscences. Using a lifeline or place list can generate a rich supply of very specific recollections.

The lifeline is simply a line divided into one- or five-year periods to which the students are invited to attach significant events, people and places. Cataloguing all the places they have lived or visited not only helps most people evoke memories of people and events, but also draws out deep feelings and buried memories associated with those places.

Exercises in visualization can help enhance the quality of the images that students recall. Visualizing real things (your kitchen, your closet, your runners, a blade of grass, a flower), fabulous things (King Kong, a city on the moon, a baby dinosaur) and people (in class, at a sports event, at a concert) draws attention not only to the technique but also to creating and remembering vivid details.

More advanced exercises invite students to call up images of people and the way they communicate non-verbally using, for example, gestures, the way they move, what they wear and how they wear it, or the possessions with which they surround themselves. Watching a TV drama with the sound turned off is an activity that can help students become more attuned to the non-verbal cues that are useful in getting across ideas.

The point of these exercises is to make it as easy and attractive as possible for students to become involved in and get satisfaction from lifewriting and its associated activities.

Making It Easy

The following ideas are suggestions for making "life-telling" and lifewriting easy. They are most effective when they are regarded as serious activities that produce results that can be retained in a portfolio as work-in-progress or used as material for follow-up group discussions.

— A photograph or picture collage (of family, of holidays, of pets, of earlier school friends, of places visited).

— A word collage, with clippings from newspapers and magazines (of useful words describing a hobby or interest, sports, ambitions, home, school).
— A word cache generated by the group to help students describe themselves both now and in the future.
— A questionnaire prepared by the group or the teacher to help jog the memory.
— Ways of examining personality types, such as the four humors, astrological signs, palm reading, Erikson's eight stages of ego development, and Myers-Briggs type indicators, or any of the various popular books on self-portrayal by personality traits.

Teachers using an exercise like this should make it clear that the purpose of these endeavors is not to gain definitive answers about personality, but to discover new descriptors and to unlock more ideas about who we are and what we do.

— Character development or history charts are also useful ways of generating ideas, especially if they are regarded as work-in-progress, with ME in the center circle, and lots of space for future ideas in large circles labeled "friends," "family," "activities," "successes," etc.

Making It Look Good

If we want students to work and re-work their initial attempts or drafts, they must value and strive for the reward that comes from doing so. By themselves, marks are not very successful in generating the kind of energy needed to inspire creative revision and refinement. Usually, the most they produce is a "corrected" copy. The innate satisfaction that comes from a job well done can be supplemented by searching for ways to showcase the lifewriting. Some simple suggestions follow:

— Display a typed or word-processed copy on the classroom bulletin board or in a school showcase, complete with a portrait of the successful author.
— Use the word-processor to publish copies using various fonts or typefaces. A computer class might be recruited to experiment with producing students' writings.
— Create a "big-book," using large sheets of chart paper and different styles of calligraphy.

— Prepare an oral presentation, perhaps involving a candle-light reading by the best readers in the class or by members of a drama class, with audio effects and background music. Videotape the presentation to provide a permanent record of the event.

Success for All

To help less proficient writers or students who are having difficulties experience the fame of authorship, it's often a good idea to provide some sample formats and models. Even a simple three-paragraph format — dealing with topics such as Me and My Family, The Places I Have Lived and What I Want to Be — can offer success to the reluctant writer who feels incapable of putting together an effective story.

Using an overhead projector to show the structure of sample autobiographies can contribute to the idea that the students are a company of lifewriting colleagues, all looking at how one of their own has tackled the matter. This technique is especially helpful if it sparks members of the group to compare their own results with those of the masters.

Finally, in making their lifewriting look great — polished and perfect — a clustering diagram of publication opportunities can be built up on a display board. With a sample piece of lifewriting at the center, the clusters can list and demonstrate alternative versions of the text — as poetry, as songs, as illustrated stories, as a résumé, an obituary, a cartoon, a picture, a play, a postcard, or even as music, dance and mime. All these forms of publication are legitimate activities for the lifewriting classroom.

Privacy or Publication?

One reservation that teachers might have about lifewriting and some of its associated activities is that students may feel pressured into disclosing matters they consider private. While some students will be open and willing to speak freely about themselves, others won't. Self-disclosure must be a voluntary act, and the teacher must emphasize this important proviso.

In our experience, this does not seem to be a major problem. In fact, individuals usually feel comfortable because of the empathy of the group, especially when the emphasis is on the individual's search to find and express meaning in a personal event. Lifewriting provides the satisfaction of facing the truth for one's own benefit, rather than as a way to upstage other members of the group.

Nevertheless, students must have the right to keep a story absolutely private, off-limits even to the teacher. Some versions of the writing portfolio have a pocket marked "private and personal" in which students can preserve and treasure such gems without fear that their privacy will be invaded. At the same time, they know they'll receive credit for finishing these stories when the contents of the portfolio are assessed.

TEACHER'S STORY: *Lifewriting with 11- to 13-Year-Olds*

KIM BENTLEY

This academic study was designed to examine whether the personal narrative, using lifewriting approaches, improved attitudes toward writing among students aged 11 to 13. Students' responses to this approach were viewed over a four-week period during which both pre-test and post-test inventories and direct observation were used to measure changes in attitudes toward writing tasks.

Conclusions and Discussion

1. The personal narrative has the power to promote a positive attitude toward writing, particularly in terms of personal engagement to task, willingness to persevere and revise, and growing interest in and response to audience reaction.
2. Personal narrative effectively improves the range of writing.

    Although lifewriting seems to be a restrictive category, the actual result tends to be that students produce a greater variety of genres such as stories, poems, factual family histories, scripts and even cartoons. The skills involved in writing personal narratives carry over into other forms of composition such as notetaking, answering exam questions and more "technical" forms of writing.
3. Lifewriting methodology promotes a more positive attitude toward writing through not only the content but also the learning strategies used.

    This positive attitude was reflected in a greater degree of talking, collaboration, and sharing and testing of ideas, as well as in improved presentation.
4. Recounting personal anecdotes has the biggest impact on students' attitudes toward writing and their view of what "being a writer of stories" means.

    This observation reinforces the basic tenet of lifewriting — that effective writing cannot be taught as a grouping of isolated elements, but must be driven by a need for self-expression within a context that is meaningful for the student. Herein lies the power of the personal narrative.

5. There was evidence that the recalling and collecting of a bank of personal memories by the students entailed much discussion with family members. This shared recollection of past family experiences led to a higher degree of interest and involvement in the task, especially by parents and grandparents.

Obviously, the involvement of parents and grandparents "in the real world" establishes a strong bond between the students' home community and their school community. The unity of purpose that exists among students, parents and teachers in the writing of personal narratives promotes a view of learning that is based on both life experiences and classroom experiences.

In conclusion, it appears that the combination of personal narratives and lifewriting is central and basic to improving attitudes toward writing and to helping students toward both self-understanding and increased understanding of their world.

. . . .

EXTENDING LIFEWRITING

ACROSS THE CURRICULUM

"Both child and teacher as storytellers are learners."

Michael Connelly and Jean Clandenin

"All writing is autobiography."

Donald Murray

Lifewriting need not always be autobiographical. When students use the power of expressive writing to focus on the world outside as well as on the self, lifewriting can become expository. It can also be a learning strategy since, as we already know, we learn best when we are able to express concepts in our own words. Personal lifewriting responses to curricular concepts bring this kind of learning into play.

Writing to Learn

Traditionally, teaching writing skills has largely been the responsibility of the English language arts instructor. However, it is clear that gaining skill and confidence as a writer helps children learn better in all areas of the curriculum. Moreover, lifewriting, while centered on the students' own ideas and experiences, isn't limited to autobiographical material. It also invites them to express their ideas about learning in all areas of the school curriculum.

Journal writing, for example, has many of the attributes of lifewriting in that it allows students the freedom to express ideas and deal with personal concerns and problems related to learning course content. Teachers in many fields assign course journals to help them follow students' learning more closely and deal with individual problems on a one-to-one basis. The subject or learning journal is also effective in raising levels of metacognition, or awareness of one's own learning processes.

Learning journals can be used effectively in the subjects shown in the following diagram. If students have different teachers for different courses, each journal may be specific to one subject. However, a single journal could become a compendium of responses to and reflections on various subjects, with specific entries being shared with the appropriate teacher.

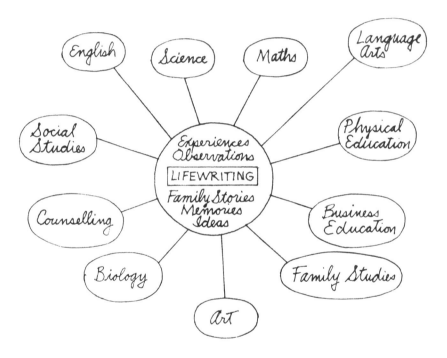

The intent is to create bridges between personal knowledge and the content of the subject, and to tap into this knowledge, encourage a reflective approach, and require the accuracy of print.

Learning journals enable students to write freely about their learning and their feelings about it. Simply being able to express frustration or confusion about trying to learn difficult material provides an opportunity to work through these negative feelings. If these messages are shared with a sympathetic teacher, the teacher can modify teaching materials and methods to help the troubled students achieve success.

Lifewriting as Exposition

Many of the subject-specific writing suggestions that follow can be used with a journal-writing program in that they all use writing to promote attitudes of enquiry, understanding and reflection. Each suggestion can also be used with an entire class or group as a freestanding activity intended to generate ideas, drafts and revised texts for a variety of purposes.

As well, the accompanying sample writing projects can be used to develop and incorporate lifewriting into a format suitable for classroom publication. Of course, as with other lifewriting activities, these projects will benefit from being combined with both the idea-generating techniques and the collaborative approach to revision and editing recommended earlier.

Lifewriting in the Fine Arts Program

Subjects like drama, painting, sculpture, pottery, music and dance encourage personal expression of ideas and emotions. The ability to respond to works of cultural diversity is also part of aesthetic and artistic development. Learning journals are places where students can respond to each other's presentations, and also interpret their own creations.

LIFEWRITING IN THE VISUAL ARTS CLASS

Because students in art classes are already expressing themselves through various visual media, it may seem unnecessary to offer them further opportunities for written or oral expression. However, language plays a vital part in both art history and criticism, and is an integral part of much of the commercial art that we encounter every day.

Student artists can use writing for recording their responses to and perceptions and interpretations of the works of others, as well as their explanations and critiques of their own works. The "artist's notebook" can combine drawing and text with ideas for further development.

In the art world, published writings take the form of reviews and critiques in magazines and exhibition catalogues and guides. These can be emulated in the art class. Students could write and share their opinions of each other's work in a guide made available to visitors attending a classroom or school exhibition. A class compendium of "Notes about the Artist" can provide the personal background to their work on display.

Sample Writing Project: A Guide to the Exhibition

The teacher encourages students to make regular entries in their journals about projects they are working on — ideas they are exploring, difficulties encountered, or aspects that seem successful. At the end of a term or semester, the artwork is displayed, accompanied by a brief guide.

To produce this "Guide to the Exhibition," students scan their journal entries, extracting several sentences or phrases that can be drawn together in a short paragraph. A class editorial committee collects these paragraphs as computer text files, edits and revises them as necessary, formats them into columns, and produces one or two copies of a pamphlet that can be laminated to accompany the classroom display.

LIFEWRITING IN THE MUSIC CLASS

Many music teachers insist that every minute of class time is needed to develop and rehearse instrumental and vocal skills. Nevertheless, performances can be enhanced by published program notes about the music to be performed or biographical notes about the performers. As well, students can record their appreciation of a particular piece of music in their journals, jotting down the feelings and memories triggered when they listened to it. Afterwards, they can share their responses with a partner or with the whole class.

Sample Writing Project: Program Notes — A Guide to the Performers

Students are invited to spend just five to 10 minutes, either at the beginning or end of a rehearsal or as a break in a longer session, collecting their thoughts and feelings in their journals. The teacher encourages them to write their "musical autobiographies," including notes about their first memories of music, their favorite pieces of music, and their memories of special musical events and incidents connected to a particular piece of music. At the end of a term or semester, students submit short paragraphs about their musical development that can be incorporated into a class "Musical Who's Who."

LIFEWRITING IN DRAMA, DANCE AND THEATER CLASSES

These artistic endeavors give rise to numerous possibilities for telling stories related to a specific dance or drama, the moods or feelings expressed, and the history of the characters involved. On a more technical level, notes and diagrams for blocking and choreography can be written, the stage manager can maintain a logbook, and the director can keep a playbook. As well, many actors find that writing out their lines helps them learn the script. Others "chunk" the play or dance into mini-scenes, describing each in their own words to catch the mood or movement.

The following project can help cast members learn more, not only about themselves but also about the people they are working with in the play or dance.

Sample Writing Project: About the Players

Students engaged in creating a classroom or school play take Polaroid pictures of each other as they appear in their roles. Using their own pictures as prompts, students draft biographical information and background notes. After sharing this information with a partner and clarifying which items need to be added or deleted, they condense the material into a 50-70 word "bio" to be included in the official program.

Lifewriting in the Sciences

LIFEWRITING IN MATH CLASS

Students are often asked to keep math journals in which they reflect on their learning and articulate the mathematical processes they've just encountered. As private communications with the teacher, the entries provide invaluable insights into their grasp of important concepts. Keeping the journal also emphasizes that understanding the process of problem-solving is just as important as reaching the right answer.

At the end of a class or when students finish a homework assignment, encourage them to spend five minutes recording their feelings about the work, difficulties they encountered and how they overcame them, or questions they want to ask the teacher. Writing to understand may also be very useful in dealing with textbook problems or puzzles in which the words may themselves be a barrier to understanding the mathematical concepts involved.

Sample Writing Project: A Little Book of Math Stories

To explore feelings and memories about learning mathematics students can be encouraged to write about their past experiences — successes or frustrations — in learning math. These stories can also include math-related experiences outside school, such as helping solve the case of the "unbalanced" family check book, working out the amount of wood needed for a deck-building project, or noticing shrinking interest payments on a savings account, as well as math-class related incidents or recollections. Anecdotes or incidents are submitted to a class editorial board, which compiles an anthology for publication.

LIFEWRITING IN THE SCIENCE CLASS

To a large extent, science involves recording observations relating to change. In this sense, it mirrors lifewriting — the recording of life as it is observed or perceived by the lifewriter.

Even in the early grades, students can be taught to record their daily observations of classroom experiments such as growing seeds, cultivating meal-worms, or hatching eggs. In the later grades, they can use their lab books like learning journals, provided space is allotted to record feelings and reactions to performing the experiments. They should also be free to comment on the scientific theories they are learning. Some of these entries might be shared with the teacher or their peers and, with elaboration and revision, may become publishable articles. Students may also be encouraged to read books on the lives of famous scientists, especially those whose autobiographies include their own personal lifewriting recorded on their journeys of discovery.

Sample Writing Project: My Life as a Scientist

Students brainstorm in groups to come up with memories of times when they have experimented outside school — training a pet, modifying an aquarium environment, changing a computer program, mixing paints to make new colors, using a magnifying glass, exploring a new chemistry, electricity or crystal radio kit received as a present, inventing an ingenious device to do a specific job, or trying to bake a cake or bread. These personal stories can be collected in a class anthology to illustrate how members of the class developed their attitudes of inquiry and observation at an earlier age.

Lifewriting in the Practical Arts

LIFEWRITING IN BUSINESS EDUCATION

Written personal expression in the business education class comes into play when, for example, students are required to develop a business plan. Research for this assignment may take the form of journal observations of a visit to a similar operation or records of an interview with an expert in the field. To increase commitment to the task, invite students to jot down how they feel about the project and how it might benefit them before they actually start to draw up the plan.

Sample Writing Project: The Personal Résumé

It is never too early for students to begin collecting the materials used for a personal résumé, in itself a form of life review. The categories of information to be included should be discussed in class — education, citizenship, interests, hobbies, work experience, travels, community involvement and so on. Using these categories to guide them, pairs of students interview each other in order to extend and select the information to be included.

An important facet of the résumé is the statement of career goals. This can begin as an informal journal entry expressing personal ambitions. Once the ideas are down on paper, students can work in pairs to refine the language and form to make it suitable for a formal résumé.

LIFEWRITING IN PHYSICAL EDUCATION

Students can use writing in many ways as part of their physical education program. The course journal can be a personal log of achievement and growth, such as a "runner's diary" that can help students set and articulate their personal goals for success. The journal also provides opportunity for analysis and reflection, whether these are about the set plays used in basketball, volleyball, football and soccer games, or about individual stroke production in golf and racket sports. Journal entries may also be fleshed out and published as records of individual and team successes, or as news stories of games lost and won.

Sample Writing Project: Our Own Sports Stars

This project gives everyone an opportunity to star in his or her own sports story. Group brainstorming would encourage all students to recall a sport-related incident from their past. Some may want to talk about special moments during team events, while others may prefer to talk about individual efforts related to skateboarding, skiing, swimming or long-distance running. Some may have memories of family pastimes at the beach or at camp. Even memories of childhood games qualify for this project.

Once everyone has settled on a personal narrative, the collaborative processes of the lifewriting group will help the writers generate ideas and details, and write and revise drafts for publication in the class booklet.

LIFEWRITING IN FAMILY STUDIES

As clothing and food are both very important to our lives, lifewriting enables students to reconstruct past experiences in order to make connections between new curriculum concepts and their previous knowledge, a fundamental principle in all learning. "Memorable Meals," for example, is a common lifewriting activity that promotes recall of a particular occasion or celebration, evoking memories of the people involved and the setting for the meal. In class, this personal story might be extended to include the menu or possibly the recipes and the preparation of the food.

Sample Writing Project: The Clothes We Wore

Everyone has memories associated with particular items of clothing worn for a special occasion. Childhood memories may also include times of tension when we were forced to wear clothes or shoes we hated. This theme provides a good topic for a group discussion that will enable every participant to share a personal story about clothing, first orally, and then as a written draft. Edited versions of these anecdotes can be collected and published as a class anthology.

Students in woodworking, metalwork or automotive shops are likely to be more interested in the practical than the theoretical. Yet there is still value in using a learning journal to express ideas and feelings about their work. Journal writing can also be a form of problem-solving, especially in designing activities that entail finding a practical solution to a construction problem. There is also value in sharing personal experiences in order to appreciate one another as individuals.

Sample Writing Project: Car Talk

The project may begin with sharing experiences in small groups, or with some students volunteering to give three-to-five-minute talks or demonstrations to the class. The theme of "Cars" provides latitude for students to talk about their first car, the first time they drove a car, taking the driving test, their first accident, their first breakdown, their first long trip by car, the cars they own, the car they would like to own, their design for an ideal car, the car of the future, their favorite car ad, etc.

As we indicated in the chapter titled "Collaboration in Lifewriting," talk is the best preparation for writing. Once all students have a story to tell, they can use drawings and pictures of cars to help them develop their story through telling it to a partner. Eventually, the stories can be drafted, edited and illustrated, and published in a class book titled Car Talk.

Lifewriting in the Humanities

Writing in social studies can be much more imaginative than the dull essays that regurgitate facts and figures culled from texts. Through lifewriting, students can bring their personal perspectives to social issues such as nationalism, the environment and ecology, racism and sexism, violence in politics and the streets, animal welfare, urban planning and law and order. Students can be encouraged to tell and write personal stories triggered by the themes being explored in class. These stories may also extend the class topic; for example, a student's story of a dangerous incident in a shopping mall could trigger discussion of and research into teenage violence and mall gangs. Either way, lifewriting enables students to express their views of the world around them.

Lifewriting also provides windows through which students can view information encountered in texts and media presentations. Already confident in the telling of personal stories, they will be better able to make the imaginative leap to tell stories that reconstruct textbook information, putting themselves in other places or historical periods to re-create the actions and feelings of people far removed in time, distance or culture.

More particularly, reconstructed life stories enable students to get beyond historical texts dominated by predominantly male political or military figures to begin to understand the lives of ordinary people in other periods. In this way, they may be able to "deconstruct" history, writing about historical events from other viewpoints — the vanquished as well as the victorious, the farmers as much as the soldiers, the female as well as the male. Multiple viewpoints can be created in imagined journals, leading to new understandings of historical events. The landing of Columbus in the New World could be seen from the perspective of the people who welcomed him, the sailors on his ships, or the wives and children who stayed at home. These forms of writing bring life to history, and may encourage students to read original historical documents such as diaries, journals and speeches.

Sample Writing Project: Innovations, Inventions and Social Change

This project may take the form of a class newspaper with stories presented in columns under headlines and students' bylines. Each group chooses a technological invention or innovation to study, and then roleplays a news conference involving the inventor or innovator and reporters. Alexander Graham Bell, for example, might be interviewed to present his views on the impact of the telephone on social relationships; Henry Ford can be asked for his views on what the mass-produced automobile would do to the landscape; and Mrs. Bloomer could be questioned about the benefits she envisions as a result of wearing trousers. Follow-up stories by other members of the group can present other views about the benefits of the invention or innovation. Edited drafts of these newspaper articles can be word-processed in columns and pasted up on large sheets of newsprint.

LIFEWRITING IN MODERN LANGUAGES

Lifewriting offers students learning a foreign language opportunities to compose sentences that are meaningful to them. For the beginner, simply completing statements such as "I am ..." or "I like ..." in the target language can be very gratifying. The power to express the self is a great motivator for students to build and learn the vocabulary and grammatical structures needed to present their own ideas. As they become more adept in the target language, they will be able to tackle the themes and topics suggested in the chapter titled "Developing Units and Programs."

Sample Writing Project: My Home

This activity may start with the students making simple line drawings of their homes, either as a sketch or a plan. They will probably need to use bilingual dictionaries to label the features of the home, or the furniture and objects in the rooms. Writing can take the form of a straightforward description, using the vocabulary generated by the drawing. A more creative approach may involve an imaginary dialogue in which the student acts as a guide to a visitor, pointing out special features. Students may also try a more challenging version of this writing activity by assigning the visitor a specific role such as that of a real estate agent or a building inspector. The teacher or a peer may help this process by adding to the draft text some questions the specific visitor might ask.

LIFEWRITING IN ENGLISH LANGUAGE ARTS

As well as helping overcome writing apprehension and developing writing skills, lifewriting builds confidence in the power of personal expression. This confidence can be the foundation of a literature program aimed at developing personal responses to the experience of reading and listening to works of literature. Individual responses to a poem, story, essay, play or novel can become springboards to group discussions that develop an appreciation for and interpretation of texts. These draft writings can be revised and published as collections of reviews or literary criticism.

Lifewriting also enables students to become creators of literature themselves. The personal stories they write can be published as class, group or individual books that deserve their place on classroom and school library shelves. Writing these stories also helps students recognize more easily the autobiographical roots of much of the fiction and poetry they read, and encourages them to try using fictional or poetic forms and styles of writing to transform their own stories. They will see that a lifewriting activity such as "Places" means creating a setting for a story; that describing a memorable person in their life means creating a character; and that writing a story with a beginning, middle and end is the same as creating a plot. They will understand that a story they write with an unexpected outcome is an example of literary irony. They will see that their own lives can be viewed as having themes, just like the novels they read. They may also decide to develop the imagery in their stories, to use a variety of figurative language, and to explore the symbolic value of the images they have created.

Sample Writing Project: Interpreting Life through Fiction

In this project, students working in groups generate a number of incidents from their experience involving some form of social conflict. Beginning with a single incident, they interpret the characters, settings and situations, creating new names and suggesting ways to extend and elaborate on the story. The aim is to produce a collaborative short story, with the usual disclaimer about resemblances between the fictional characters and real persons. As the short story develops through various drafts, students will be able to use their knowledge of literary techniques to develop imagery and symbols. Dialogue will be created to express human interactions. Students may also experiment with different endings to see which is the most effective.

Completed stories can be exchanged between groups for interpretation and response. The finished stories can be published as a bound, word-processed text, complete with a hard cover, and become part of the classroom library.

LITERATURE AS LIFEWRITING

When students have had the experience of creating their own life stories as memoirs, anecdotes and family histories, they will better appreciate authors who have raised lifewriting to a high art in various forms of autobiography and travelogue. They will understand how professional writers must deal with problems of self-representation and identity, and with what constitutes truth when they are telling their own stories as they see them. They will enjoy the autobiographies and memoirs (even if ghost-written) of their favorite sports, movie, or rock heroes. Above all, they will appreciate the values of personal expression in the diaries of people such as Anne Frank or Robert F. Scott, the Antarctic explorer. Autobiographical stories of adventure, travel and discovery can be read both for their general interest as well as their historical value.

Once students enter the realm of published personal experiences, they can be introduced to famous people's stories related to every area of the school curriculum. The following autobiographies are merely suggestions. Students can scour the library to find the life stories of famous or infamous people who interest them.

Visual Arts: Luis Bunuel — *My Last Sigh*
Music: Joan Baez — *And a Voice to Sing with*
Theater: George Burns — *All My Best Friends*
Math: S.M. Ulam — *Adventures of a Mathematician*
Science: Isaac Asimov — *In Memory Yet Green*
Business: Thomas T. Watson — *Father, Son and Co.: My Life at IBM and Beyond*
Physical education: Howard Cosell — *I Never Played the Game*
Family studies: Hardy Amies — *Still Here*
Technical education: Orville Wright — *How We Invented the Airplane*
Social studies: W. John Hackwell — *Diving to the Past: Recovering Ancient Wrecks*
Modern languages: Witold Gombrowicz — *Diary: Vol. 2*
English language arts: Beverly Cleary — *A Girl from Yamhill: A Memoir*

Lifewriting and Career and Personal Planning

Some people know from early on what they want to be and do. We have all known those who want to be nurses, teachers, engineers or athletes. These people have endless opportunities to develop the ideal résumé for themselves — a forward-looking exercise that can form the basis of planning. They can also write about what they think life is like in their chosen profession, as well as hear, read and retell the stories of people already working in that field.

For others who are still developing their career choices, drafting alternative career paths not only reinforces the idea that a little planning can help when selecting appropriate courses and gaining related experience, but also introduces the idea that they can make choices and exercise control over their future.

In general, career planning of any sort enhances our personal understanding of our ambitions, strengths and weaknesses. It also helps us understand other aspects of planning for a future job — keeping informed, networking, finding a fit between our skills and talents and possible career choices, and exploring the fit between our self-image and the public image of a particular career. At a more reflective level, this kind of planning can lead to the recognition that acquiring specific qualifications or a particular job is not the ultimate goal, especially when we realize that the future may actually hold a series of jobs or even career changes. This realization can lead to exciting speculations about possible life situations 10, 20 or even 30 years down the road.

Sample Writing Project: Ten Years from Now

Writing about "My Brilliant Career" or "My Fabulous Life" offers endless possibilities. A more realistic approach is to write the story of what one might be doing in 10 years, including the events, training and experience that have occurred in the meantime. For those who have difficulty writing, constructing an agreed-upon future résumé can be a worthwhile group exercise, with students contributing detailed information under headings such as Present Position, Experience, Training and Education, and Special Abilities and Interests.

TEACHER'S STORY: *The Inside Me and the Outside Me*

ROB GRANTHAM

This unit began as a science unit on the human body. What evolved was an integrated theme involving science, language arts, fine arts and social studies as part of a cohesive learning experience. The Inside Me focused on scientific information, while The Outside Me encompassed the other curriculum areas. These activities occupied the 10- to 12-year-old students at Denman Island Elementary School for three months and met with great success.

The scientific content was a study of the systems and processes of the human body. The students' prior knowledge was built upon through in-depth videos, models, charts, readings, research and discussions. This information was brought together as every student created a life-sized poster of her or his inner body using a variety of artistic techniques.

Our reading program for this unit focused on Jean Little's *Mine for Keeps*, the story of a young girl with cerebral palsy, a novel that fit in well with our science theme because it illustrates the importance of the brain and the nervous system. More important, the book helped us understand the situations of people with disabilities.

The writing component of The Outside Me consisted of various tasks that invited the children to explore and express their own history and uniqueness as a person. The students wrote poems introducing themselves, drew one-metre time-lines on which they plotted and illustrated the major events of their lives, and wrote of their family history. A major writing assignment paralleled one of the themes from *Mine for Keeps* — the protagonist's gradual progress toward independence. Each student created a web titled "Changes That Have Happened in My Life" and then wrote a detailed story of the change she or he found to be the most interesting and important. Some of these stories were read as part of a radio broadcast about this project.

Finally, each student created a life-sized "Outside Me" poster that emphasized what they felt was unique and special about themselves. We stapled the posters back-to-back with the Inside Me posters, and stuffed them with newspapers to create a three-dimensional "person." We displayed these for the community at our Christmas celebration as a spectacular expression of the students' individualities, and a good record of their ideas and learning.

. . . .

LIFEWRITING

AND COMPUTERS

"I must write, I must write at all cost. For writing is more than living, it is being conscious of living."

Ann Morrow Lindbergh

This chapter has been designed with a typically modern classroom in mind, one that's equipped with one or two basic computers, a printer and possibly a modem connection to the outside world of information and communication networks. In addition, we have assumed that students will have some access to a school computer lab where they may be able to use more sophisticated hardware with a larger variety of programs.

Of course, there are still too many classrooms without this kind of modern technology, even though many students have their own computers at home. But at the other end of the equipment spectrum, one newly built high school for 1,200 students in the Ottawa area is equipped with about 300 computers. In this school, English classes meet in a room where every student sits in front of a personal computer, using a wide range of Windows-based software, including programs for multimedia composition with CD-ROM software and laserdisk players. Even in an older, inner-city secondary school, the transition English as a second language classes meet to study social studies and science in a multimedia room that provides every student with a network of personal computers linked to the computer, CD-ROM drive, scanner and laserdisk player on the teacher's desk.

But this chapter is not about technology. It's about how a single basic computer can enhance lifewriting activities. And if an inexpensive modem connected to a telephone line is added to the mix, writing activities can be exchanged with students in other classrooms, across the city, across the nation, or even around the world. Electronic mail provides new audiences and possibilities for exchanging stories, and electronic bulletin boards offer students the opportunity to network with other people with similar or specialized interests.

But why bother with the computer at all? Don't some people feel it actually gets in the way of putting thoughts down on paper? Maybe so, but everyone should at least be given the chance to try writing with a computer, and to see if their needs can be accommodated by any of the powerful software packages designed to take some of the drudgery out of writing. Once they've had this chance, many people find that the computer provides a stimulating and engaging path to effective composition.

The computer can also serve as a magnet, drawing partners or groups into cooperative keyboarding, composing, correcting and revising as they gather round to read the text that appears on the screen. It also lures individuals into carefully monitoring what is being transmitted from keyboard to screen, and into playing with the shape and size of the composition depicted.

The ease with which neophyte lifewriters can use the computer to produce good-looking work is a real plus for the technology. At the end of drafting, revising, correcting and editing, there is a presentable — and often impressive — text. This almost instant reward is frequently denied the pen-and-pencil composer. There is also the additional benefit that any further corrections, suggestions, ideas, and images can be incorporated without the tedious task of hand writing or typing the whole piece all over again. Couple word processing with desktop publishing capabilities, and every lifewriter can become a self-publisher. The computer can also be used to store and process information about the people, places, times and events in one's life that are the stuff of all life stories.

Clearly, with these advantages, and with its status as a very contemporary medium, the computer can attract students who have had difficulty with traditional pen-and-paper methods of writing. It offers them a fresh start, giving them and other users opportunities to shift blocks of text, call on spelling or grammar checkers for assistance, find alternative ways of expressing their ideas through a built-in thesaurus, or use a split screen to compare two texts or two versions of the same text simultaneously. Furthermore, at the publishing stage, writers can experiment with different layouts, fonts and type-faces, and use boxes, lines and illustrations to create an excit-ing, attractive text.

It's interesting to note that reading and writing on a com-puter can also help some ESL learners assimilate the left-to-right and top-to-bottom sequence of text in English.

Keyboarding

Even very young students are quick to figure out how to use the keyboard to write their stories. They learn more quickly if they are encouraged to leap in and start using it right away, rather than waiting for instructions on keyboarding tech-niques. While their slow, hunt-and-peck efforts may seem painful and ponderous at first, primary teachers are likely to find that emergent writers are able to locate letters on the keyboard in much less time than it takes them to laboriously print them using paper and pencil. Once youngsters have begun to use the computer, the drive to work the machine accelerates their learning. In any case, there is often a student expert in the class who is ready and willing to help the begin-ner, exemplifying the effectiveness of pairing learners with experts.

Some teachers prefer to plan a few brief class sessions to introduce keyboarding activities. They provide each student with a full-sized copy of a keyboard to introduce them to the home and function keys, and assign activities that prepare them to use all 10 fingers. Many use a set dictation piece to alert neophytes to the computer's capabilities and the user's mistakes.

The aim is to get students writing quickly, unencumbered by protracted instructions about booting up, loading pro-grams or keyboarding skills. The teacher makes sure that the computer is up and running with a word-processing program and the student writer takes it from there. Later, students can be shown how to save and retrieve texts on their own individ-ual disks. Keyboarding programs that teach the keyboard through a number of challenging games can also be made available later.

Introductory Activities

To keep the focus on writing, a simple round-robin game can be used to break the ice. Each student takes a turn at the computer workstation, completing a few basic sentences, such as *Hello, I am... I like...*. Other sentence beginnings can be introduced day by day: *My favorite TV show is..., I think that..., I used to...* and *Red is the color of...*. These sentence starters can be posted on charts near the computer so students can type them out and complete them independently or with a partner while other class activities are going on.

Students may choose to compose their messages on paper beforehand, or rehearse them in their heads before they get their turn on the computer. At the conclusion of each exercise, the results can be printed out and the ideas shared with the whole class. Doing this has two immediate effects: the students identify and learn to correct their own word-processing mistakes, and they strive to emulate the successful efforts of their peers.

To move beyond these short introductory class texts, the following data collection and writing aids provide rewarding starts:

— Biographical probes: Who are you? Where have you lived? What do you like doing during the day? In the evenings? On weekends? During holidays?
— Random thoughts: Things I like, things I dislike, What I would change about ..., If I ruled the world, I would ..., If I were given the job of changing education 10 years from now, I would ...
— Template completion: Templates, a set of on-screen prompts provided by the teacher, can range from a series of headings and sub-headings under which students fill in thoughts or information through to a framework of sentence starters that students complete. When completed, these templates generate passable and coherent pieces of writing.

A template approach to a first piece of lifewriting offers success. Initially, students approach it as a co-authoring assignment but end up assuming ownership of the writing. The headings of a "My Life" essay seem to work especially well. Although many variations on this theme are possible, the following pattern has worked successfully with adult students. It can be used with younger students to create a fictional piece, or the headings can be changed to suit the life experiences of a particular group of students.

My Life

My Family Background
— Grandparents, parents
— Brothers and sisters
— Places where my family has lived

My Life So Far
— Earliest memories, pre-school
— School
— Other activities, interests
— Special occasions, happenings, visits

My Future
— My expectations, hopes, ambitions
— My fantasies

In addition to helping students learn to use a computer, other activities, such as free writing, timed writing or assigned writing, help students get words down on the screen just as they would on paper. Any of these activities can also be carried out with the screen turned off, or with the brightness turned down, so that text is recorded as invisible writing, freeing the students from the screen and enabling them to concentrate on their thoughts and on the keyboard.

If computer time is limited, as it probably is for most classes, much of this idea-generating and initial drafting work can be done on paper and transposed to the computer at scheduled times. The problem with this approach is that it does not capitalize on the novelty of composing directly on the computer. However, students may take more interest in what and how they are writing, knowing that the results are to be transferred to the computer and printed out.

A number of commercial computer software programs are specifically designed for student writers. Most of them provide verbal and visual prompts that help students develop word caches or lists of ideas; others use open-ended questions, sentence beginnings or sentence frames, and in some cases, try to build on the students' responses. The advantage of software like this is that students work directly with the computer and develop their own sense of mastery. However, these programs are intended for individuals who have ready access to a computer over long periods, something that isn't possible in many classrooms or labs. Nevertheless, the software can be a useful addition to a resource center or remedial learning station, and can be used in a computer lab in combination with pen-and-paper activities.

Computer Collaboration

There are a number of exciting ways to involve students in cooperative composition using the computer. The interview partnership is very effective, with one student acting as the interviewer who asks questions about a partner's life and interests. As both students sit at the computer, the interviewer types in a question, then turns the keyboard over to the subject for a response. It's also possible for a third person to act as an intermediary between both the interviewer and subject, typing both the questions and the responses into the computer as they are dictated. When the screen is filled, everyone involved can study the results and re-work the ideas as the subject's "autobiography." Provided that the subject is satisfied with the accuracy and completeness of the information, the final text can be saved on disk. Then students can exchange roles and repeat the process until all the participants have created an autobiographical story. The teacher can speed up the process by having on hand a series of resource cards with trigger questions, beginnings, endings and formats that can be used as necessary.

The following collaborative activities work well:

— A class "Who's Who?" developed by a group to include short biographies of every member of the class. An "All about ..." portrait of one member of the group compiled, with the subject's approval, from contributions made by other group members.

— Fantasy autobiographies or life-stories about each member of the group telling of their achievements in the future.
— Résumé writing.
— Lifewriting clinics during which an "expert" group helps a subject produce an autobiographical piece by offering advice on content and form.

Cooperation comes into play not only when students are writing collaboratively, but also when someone helps others use the keyboard, format and illustrate a text, or manage the computer files. There are always a few experienced users in each class who need little encouragement to help in this way. But there must always be room for individual differences in adapting to the computer. Some writers need time and space for rehearsing their ideas in their head, for solo writing, for playing with pen and paper or simply for "doodling." There is no advantage to be gained from forcing changes in these individual writing behaviors.

Although research suggests that some students write more on the computer than on paper and also write more in a group than alone, there may be difficulties with the development of the writer's individual voice and sense of ownership, especially if the quality of the jointly produced text varies significantly from an individual's capabilities. Even so, the collaborative approach is stimulating, educational and rewarding in all settings, and is all the more so when a computer is used.

Revision

There are two great advantages to revising on the computer. First, it's easy. Second, there is a distance or separation between the writer and text that makes it easier for the writer to consider her or his efforts objectively.

Although some shifting around is possible with scissors and paste, a handwritten draft is difficult to revise because large-scale changes and continual revisions or editing are just too much trouble. The computer is forgiving in that spelling, vocabulary, and grammatical forms can be identified and changed with ease. Because the printed product looks so good, so much more professional than a handwritten copy, however, there is a danger that the revision may be superficial. Nevertheless, collaboration, feedback from other students and the teacher, and reflective reading by the writer can combat the first impression of near-perfection that crisp, clean hard copy can give.

The distance intrinsic in text on a screen makes it easier for everyone involved to give a piece of writing the closer scrutiny it deserves. Even the writer feels somewhat removed from the words on the monitor. It's almost as if they are a different product because they appear in a different medium. An example of this is our reaction when we read through a letter we've written after it's been typed and printed. We seem to see the message with new eyes. So, too, when lifewriters and their peers see work on the screen. It attracts an interest in re-reading that is often absent when a text is handwritten, especially because making changes to handwritten copy can be dauntingly time-consuming. Making changes or corrections means much less work when word-processing is involved. The following revision-based activities can be used with a large group or the whole class:

— The teacher models revision strategies on her own writing drafts, using a computer projection plate in conjunction with an overhead projector to display the computer screen for all to see.
— Distribute practice pieces for groups to revise. Their revised drafts can be typed into the computer for comparison with the original, or each group can produce a revised version directly onto an overhead transparency for comparison and discussion.
— Work with the class to generate general questions that a group or individual can ask when revising (e.g., What's the focus of this piece? Does the opening show this and catch the reader's attention? Does the writer keep to the point? Are illustrations helpful? Does the ending satisfy the reader?).
— Invite writers to present a commentary on why changes were made, what problems they needed to solve, and what sections they are still dissatisfied with. This shar-

ing helps other writers and also engenders a reflective approach in the writers themselves.

As mentioned earlier, a number of computer programs are designed specifically to assist with writing. Many word-processing programs now include a spell-check, a thesaurus and a grammar and punctuation checker. Programs like these can reduce writing apprehension. Some can even keep track of recurring spelling errors, word repetitions and atypical punctuation patterns peculiar to the user, providing opportunities for new learning and remediation.

Obviously, these programs have limitations, such as an inability to distinguish between homophones, but even these can be turned to teaching advantage. The fact that the messages and prompts simply provide signals to the user rather than the correct answers keeps the writer alert and in control. Some incidental learning about how our language works may also take place as users begin to grasp the logic or patterns behind the programs' responses to their work.

Publication

Although it's easy to print good-looking work using a computer, not all pieces of writing need to — or should be — taken to this final stage. Not all need to be displayed, shared or published. Some are simply experiments, some may be stored to be retrieved for later development, and some should simply be abandoned. Most early drafts will be retained in the writer's portfolio or as computer files on the student's personal disk. Still, every student should have some published writing that demonstrates progress, originality or valuable ideas.

Especially at the beginning of a lifewriting program, it is essential that all students have an opportunity to share at least one finished story with members of the group or the whole class. The desktop publishing capacity of the computer provides such sophisticated publishing possibilities that students' texts can be presented in print that nearly matches the quality of traditional typesetting. Published work can appear in public outlets such the following:

- A writer's corner or display cabinet in the school's entrance hall.
- A newsletter sent to parents, or in a school magazine.
- A class book, bound and illustrated by the students and placed on the classroom or library shelves.
- An individual book, with the student's story printed out and bound in cardboard covers, complete with a title page, classroom imprint, acknowledgments, illustrations and a biographical note on the author.

Using a computer for writing has a number of built-in rewards, but the final goal of some sort of real publication gives students' stories a value that far transcends regular written classroom or homework exercises and assignments.

Surprisingly, there is more personal testimony than reliable research on the effectiveness of writing with a computer. What is evident, however, is that it attracts students eager for a break from conventional classroom activities and helps them feel they are a part of the world of burgeoning technology. Moreover, it encourages independence, empowers students to take control of their work, and promotes the writer's engagement with the text. It also serves as a center for self-directed activity, fostering students' sense of achievement and pride in the published products.

Communicating beyond the Classroom

A modem connection opens up the classroom to the whole world of communications networking known as the Information Highway, including electronic mailing systems — e-mail — and bulletin boards — BBSs. This cyberspace highway is a two-way street; students can contribute their knowledge and experience to a network as well as receive information from it. Sharing personal narratives with other classes in other countries becomes an immediate possibility, as does the opportunity to share in a joint venture with other schools throughout the world.

One recent Internet project that originated in California recruited students from more than a hundred schools around the world to keep hour-by-hour diaries of their experiences on a specific day. The results were posted on an electronic bulletin board, enabling participants to compare their experiences.

At a simpler level, one school or classroom can pair up with another, whether in the same city, province or state, or separated by thousands of miles. In one project, students in California shared their ideas and experiences with others in Alaska, exploring the cultural effects of their very different environments. In another sea-to-sea project, students in Vancouver shared their stories with classes in Halifax. Before long, community, provincial and state learning networks will make this sort of exciting interchange a possibility for all schools.

This kind of interchange began more than 500 years ago when Gutenberg's invention of the printing press brought books and news sheets within reach of the general public. The quintessential human inclination to share life stories face-to-face moved into another dimension as this new medium offered the possibility of connecting with audiences across space and time. Five hundred years later, with communication theorist Marshall McLuhan's postulation that the medium is the message in mind, it is interesting to consider how lifewriting itself will be transformed by electronic media.

It can be argued that when the computer is used simply as an extension of handwritten lifewriting, it is serving as little more than a very sophisticated typewriter. However, technology does not stand still, and a variety of current developments may change the nature of lifewriting.

We have already mentioned briefly the value of e-mail, a form of electronic communication that enables the lifewriter to send a message instantly and cheaply to any one of the millions of e-mail addresses around the world. The message may be no more than a few words typed directly on the screen, or it may be an entire story attached as a file to the e-mail message. Moreover, although the story is directed to one recipient, copies of it can be forwarded to any number of other e-mail addresses. Transmission takes only a few seconds; whether the recipients actually read what is sent depends on the vagaries of the human condition. Nevertheless, the act of sending a story into cyberspace is a form of publishing in that the lifewriter has submitted a slice of life history to readers around the world for them to enjoy and judge.

The computer's ability to reach audiences is matched by the audience's ability to respond very quickly via the same medium. So now the possibility exists for electronic lifewriting to become more like a face-to-face dialogue, with the added twist that we are no longer limited to the relatively few people we can talk to in a day. Theoretically, we can talk to the whole world.

Electronic bulletin boards or user groups are also available to lifewriters via a modem link. They offer possibilities for making contact with a group of writers who share a common interest and offer each other support no matter what distance separates them. Through the information highway anyone can join a user group by responding to messages posted on the bulletin board, and can also contribute their own stories and messages. These groups usually have a moderator who screens contributions to ensure that only those compatible with the aims of the group are actually posted on the bulletin board.

Finally, the tremendous advances in multimedia communications mean that the electronic lifewriter is no longer confined to typing text on a screen. Already it is possible to transmit stories complete with colored pictures and audio-video components. Future lifewriters may well be telling their stories with the help of a video camera and a storehouse of audio and video clips. Or we may see a return to storytelling as the human voice becomes the preferred means of communicating with and via the computer. It's already possible to simply tell certain computers what we want them to do. Chances are that in the near future we will no longer have to sit in front of a screen, interacting with the computer by means of a keyboard or a mouse. We will be composing our life stories by thinking aloud. Our spoken texts will be recorded digitally so that they can be reviewed, revised, stored or shared at our convenience.

Whatever the future holds, and whatever new writing tools are at our disposal, one thing will remain the same: even though the medium may change or even be the message, the uncovering of memories and ideas and the accompanying processes of reflecting and re-creating will still be the moving forces behind our telling and writing of our life stories.

TEACHER'S STORY: *Writing with Computers in a Primary Class*

ANDREA LEE

As part of my course work toward my master's degree, I decided to introduce my class of seven- and eight-year-olds to lifewriting. I understood that lifewriting implied "a sense of expression of life and identity," where writing about our lives would enable us to "taste life twice" and "persuade ourselves that life is eternal." I have carried these words with me since completing the course myself, and decided to share them, and an experience with lifewriting, with the children in my class.

I have discovered that an anthology of writing from each member of the class makes a wonderful end-of-year gift. It records what the children have achieved to date and may be revisited in the future. This year I decided that a book based on a lifewriting experience would be even more appropriate.

For our theme, I chose "A Sense of Place." Each child wrote a personal list of special places in her or his life. After sharing the lists with partners, students drew a small picture or "snap-shot" of one special place. Then they generated a series of shorter lists of sights, sounds, tastes and textures to describe their special place, and the people and feelings associated with it. These words and phrases formed the basis of our individual stories.

We drafted the stories first with pencil and paper, then used our classroom computer to process the stories. This program gave us a clear print-out of the first draft of each story. Then the children, with my help, revised, elaborated on and edited each story, and eventually put them together between covers in our class book. On the last day of school, I presented each child with a personal copy of the book. I think it is a testament to the success of our endeavor that we spent a good part of that last morning reading our stories and signing our names in each other's books where our story was located.

When I try this project again, I will share the first line of Isak Dineson's book, *Out of Africa*: "I once had a farm in Africa." Dineson reminds us that one special place can be a lifetime of memories.

. . . .

EVALUATING LIFEWRITING

"Nostalgia ain't what it used to be."

Anonymous

"Nostalgia is like a grammar lesson; you find the present tense and the past perfect."

Anonymous

Some teachers find it difficult to grade students' performance or participation in a lifewriting unit, whether as part of an English program or as one aspect of writing ability assessment. If lifewriting forms the core of the writing program, it is obvious that the teacher and the students will want some sort of mark. The old adage seems to hold — what counts is what is counted.

The necessity of assigning a grade is not an insurmountable problem, although doing so does seem to enforce the idea we've been trying to get away from — that writing done in school is simply a means of obtaining marks. Admittedly, too, it would seem to require the wisdom of a Solomon to separate individual contributions from group efforts when evaluating lifewriting.

The following are various ways of evaluating students' writings. These five simple strategies can provide data to use for reporting on students' progress as required by a particular school system.

1. When a piece of writing must be produced for a mark under examination conditions, the selection of topics can include several previously generated in the lifewriting unit. Students can be asked to write an autobiographical or biographical sketch or an illustrative narrative on one of those topics, and the product can be marked by the conventional criteria used in the system. The focus here is

not on the amount of time spent in class generating ideas alone or in a group, or on the revisions made or assistance given, but on the final written product achieved in the test situation. This product is the test of what has been learned as a result of all the preliminary efforts.

2. If grades are based on a term's or year's work, the student might be asked to present the best three or more pieces of work in the writing portfolio to the teacher for assessment. In asking for the student's "best" work, the point is to evaluate how well the student can do, not to assign a mark on the basis of rejected work or failed attempts.

3. A student's complete portfolio can be used to assess the term's or year's work. The mark can be based on a composite of various criteria, including the variety and quantity of the drafts and finished pieces, and the evidence of the student's development as a writer.

4. Because one goal of lifewriting is to encourage students to take responsibility for their own learning, it is desirable to involve them in the evaluation and assessment process. An assessment sheet linked to the contents of an individual's writing folio helps achieve this. On it, the student lists the titles of all finished first drafts, together with the titles of pieces shared more formally with a partner or members of a response group, and the titles of all pieces published in other forms. Marks can be awarded in each category and, when assigning a grade, the teacher need only check the contents of the portfolio against the summary sheet and add up the marks.

We have successfully used the assessment sheet on the following page with older adolescents and adults. It can, however, be adapted to fit a variety of situations.

If the lifewriting program has been successful, the teacher will have enough material to produce marks. In fact, he may very well have many more samples than are typically produced as regular language arts or English class assignments. Still, it is important to see lifewriting as a process that leads to improvement in communication by empowering and engaging students, rather than as a way of giving — or getting — marks.

The lifewriting teacher should never be just a marker or evaluator. Her primary purpose is to encourage and promote development. As the chart on the following page indicates, the formative evaluation or "progress report" approach achieves this purpose. The column titled "What?" includes actions the teacher and group members can take to determine a student's

---

Name_____

Assessment of the Lifewriting Unit

Please note: There are many ways to evaluate writing. Professional authors may take into account the number of copies of a book that are sold, or how many times a book is reprinted, re-published in a new edition, or translated into other languages. It is also valuable for an author to sell the film rights to a story, or achieve fame through appearances on talk shows. Generally, the professional author needs to make money, so that one method of evaluation is to count how much money the author makes through writing.

In school, however, we depend on feedback from our readers — other students, the teacher, friends or family members. Their responses can help us feel that our ideas are valuable and worth putting into print. We also need marks or grades to recognize our achievement.

In this lifewriting unit, we wish to recognize the value of the stories we have drafted for ourselves, the stories that we share with members of the group or the whole class, and stories that are published in individual, group or class books. Therefore, you will evaluate your own stories according to the following scale:

First, or rough, drafts of a story...   1 point each
Stories read or shared with a group...   3 points each
Published stories in polished format...   5 points each
Author's note...   2 points
    (To a maximum of 20 points for the unit)

On the back of this sheet, please list the titles of stories included in each category. Remember to save all your drafts and finished copies in your writing portfolio.

---

progress. The column titled "Why?" includes reasons for these actions and the column titled "How?" offers suggestions for carrying out the action indicated in the first column.

Formative Evaluation of Student Writing		
What?	*Why?*	*How?*
Respond to ideas	Provide support and encouragement	Oral comments
Praise strengths, originality, creativity, arguments, etc. Identify possible audience and writing forms	Show potential value of first drafts	Writing conferences Written responses from peers
Suggest publishing outlets	Help students decide whether to preserve as is, or revise for publication	Provide models and examples
Show where additions or deletions are possible Show where ideas are weak or confused Give a reader's response to a work in progress	Help students revise	Peer editing: partner or group conference Read and return with editor's note
Scan writing for superficial errors	Help students edit	Arrange for proofreading help from peers Provide models of presentations
Scan writing for presentation format	Help students present or publish	Provide an editing center with reference books and other writing resources
Decide whether a piece of writing meets the standards of the audience	Encourage high presentation standards	Establish class editorial board

As you read the chart from top to bottom, notice how the focus of the evaluation shifts from the writer's ideas, or the content, to decisions about the overall structure, the intended readership, and the form of publication. Only as a piece of writing nears completion does attention shift to the mechanics of writing as part of a final proofreading and clean-up. In practice, most grammar, spelling, punctuation and capitalization errors will be shaken out of the text during the revision and editing process.

What about Mechanics?

Before we explore the answer to this question, we should make our starting position clear:

— A knowledge of grammar does not by itself improve writing.
— Students who do have a detailed knowledge of rules and usage do not necessarily use this in their writing.
— Teacher's corrections noted on students' papers do not often improve their grammar.

So what's a teacher to do?

First, one of the most effective approaches is to help students develop an "ear" for what sounds right. This intuitive sense of grammar is fostered in lifewriting classes by the reading aloud of stories, and the listening, sharing and helping that occurs. In this kind of environment, students can function without rules for most drafting — if they are in a setting in which English is the home language. In addition, the emphasis on collaboration provides the opportunity to consult peers who are "expert" in such things as verb agreement or commas (and will likely become even more expert as they are appealed to for answers!). And finally, in the exploratory language setting that lifewriting encourages, there is always the teacher to give individual help. So the teacher should keep the focus on "Does it sound right?" and if the answer is no, then encourage the student to ask for expert help.

Second, with its stress on revising and polishing, the program shifts from the teacher's "Here are the rules of grammar" to the student's "What skills do I need to do this right?" Students will benefit more from assistance or instruction in solving a specific problem than from any general introduction to mechanics or grammar. Mini-lessons designed to meet a specific need work best.

However, there are a number of ways in which teachers can address mechanics that merit attention:

1. Keep a mechanics record for the class. Use broad headings like Paragraphing, Punctuation and Agreement of Subject and Verb to record occurrences of problems in these areas. The list can be more specific, with headings like Subject-Predicate Agreement, Pronoun-Antecedent Agreement, Sentence Fragments and Punctuation Misuse that are appropriate to the age and background of the class. Use this record to select topics for class or small group mini-lessons.

2. If you mark students' writing in detail, ask them to keep their own individual record of errors, and use this as the basis for an individual conference, a small-group lesson, or self-directed exercises in a textbook or writing manual.

3. Make a priority list of mechanics and grammar rules that you want students to attend to during the revising and editing stage. Do not make this a comprehensive list, but rather focus on a few major elements you want students to pay the most attention to.

4. Draw up a simple, general list of items (with examples) for use by the editing groups or at the editing stage. This list will provoke questions that give the teacher opportunities to plan mini-lessons.

5. Prepare a final checklist for individuals to attach to the cover of their portfolios. This list should be short; it loses its effectiveness if it tries to cover too many problems, or is too vague or troublesome to use.

6. Develop a help directory. This can include references to the appropriate pages in the textbook or a grammar handbook, to the class experts, or to a computer program that can check spelling or grammatical constructions. Again, the signposts should be simple and the information easy to follow.

7. Conduct brief training sessions for students who want to know more about the mechanics of language.

8. Direct students to established writers who have tackled the sort of problem they are struggling with; for instance,

suggest a play script or short story replete with dialogue to see how quotation marks are used. In short, foster the reading of literature to develop further that intuitive sense — the writer's inner voice.

Teachers are better prepared to help the students if they attempt to assess a student's grasp of knowledge or skills at certain points in the lifewriting program. Summative evaluation enables the teacher to gauge the effectiveness of her teaching by examining what the students have learned. This type of evaluation, summarized in the following chart, is familiar to students accustomed to having their writing marked and graded for report cards.

Achievement scores can help students measure their abilities and perhaps make predictions about their future success

Summative Evaluation of Student Writing		
What?	*Why?*	*How?*
Student participation in writing activities	Assess student's attitudes to writing	Classroom observation Self-evaluation
Quantity and variety of writing projects attempted	Assess student's drafting skills	Assessment scale of student's writing portfolio
Ability to shape and change a piece of writing	Assess student's editing ability	Comparison of draft and finished copy of a selected piece of writing
Test-piece given as an editing exercise	Assess ability to help other students as co-editor	Observe partners working together
Quantity and variety of writings presented or published at an acceptable standard	Assess student's overall writing ability	Class records of writings edited and presented or published

in the academic or business world. In a school setting, it is possible to establish and use a system of summative evaluation to measure achievement in lifewriting that can be of some help to students. The teacher can make comparative evaluations about the quantity and quality of pieces of lifewriting generated during a term or semester, and eventually convert these scores to an overall grade.

Actually, some students may feel disappointed or a little cheated if all their writing is not collected for marking and grading. Nevertheless, the teacher must resist being lured into playing the role of judge and "executioner." Writings will be read by the teacher, of course, as well as by others, but mainly within the framework of works in progress. As long as readers respond to individual pieces of writing, going along with minor imperfections but seeing the potential value, then the writer can be encouraged. Comments and criticisms offered within this framework are accepted as helpful advice.

Viewed in this light, no piece of writing can be judged a failure. A work in progress is writing in a state of becoming, and it will always have the potential to be improved by the writer. Writing is finished only when it is published or put away for preservation. Publication, like virtue, is its own reward. An honest response from a sympathetic reader is the best evaluation any writer can receive.

Even if lifewriting is part of an actual college or school course for which an overall grade must be assigned, the grading system should recognize all aspects of the lifewriting program. Students deserve an assessment of their pre-writing and revision efforts, as well as of their final products. The first column of the chart on page 90 shows the aspects of an instructional program that can be measured during a semester or reporting period when preparing an assessment of performance in specific writing tasks.

However, as we have stated time and again, individual success in the typical lifewriting workshop is measured, not by the reward of a teacher's grades, but by what the lifewriters feel they have gained from the activities. For some people, the written products are the most important proof of the success of the workshop. And even the accumulation of notes, scribbles, lists and false starts in the lifewriter's portfolio also provides a satisfactory indication of accomplishment. In the end, it is the participant's perception that is the real assessment of achievement. The principal aim of formative evaluation is to provide the help and encouragement each participant needs to see and feel the real value of reviewing and recording life's experiences.

The Writing Portfolio

The writing portfolio, like an artist's portfolio, is meant to contain works in progress, first attempts, jottings, work abandoned, work that did not come off, and sketches set aside for development later. It is amazing how quickly these fragments and pieces accumulate, giving the writer a sense of progress and a feeling of confidence about writing. The portfolio provides a store of material to be worked on or used as further inspiration. It also gives the teacher evidence of a student's quantitative and qualitative development and provides material for diagnosis and counseling.

Finally, reader response is the most valuable assessment any published author can receive. Accordingly, any of the suggestions for sharing work with others — class books, newsletters, e-mail messages, and so on — can also be seen as opportunities for real, meaningful evaluation.

TEACHER'S STORY: *If I Had My Life to Live Over*

THE BROCK HOUSE WRITERS

"This anthology is published by the Brock House Writers and is dedicated to the Grade 7 students at Bayview Community School. Our writings are partly memories of what our lives have been, and what they might be if we were to live them over today. In presenting them, we hope not only that you may find them interesting, but that you may also receive some ideas as to how you might prepare yourselves for life in the 21st century. It will be your century. The world will be your oyster this time. We sincerely hope that you will make the most of it. Seize the day!"

The Brock House Writers

This introduction was part of a project organized by Irene Ovenden, a member of a seniors' writing group at the Brock House Recreation Centre in Vancouver. Members of the writing group visited Rick Sinclair's class of 12- and 13-year-olds at the nearby Bayview Community School and shared stories they had written about their lives, focusing on the theme "If I Had My Life to Live Over." Many of today's seniors were not aware in the past of what they might have done with their lives. For example, many women assumed that it was their place to be at home. They never considered entering the work force in any of the professions available to them at that time, and never dreamed of the many more opportunities that are available today.

By sharing their stories with the students, the Brock House Writers hoped to show not only how they had achieved their present place in society, but also, given today's opportunities, what they would like to achieve in the future. They hoped to inspire the students to make the most of the educational opportunities opening up to them. They especially wanted the students to see that living is a life-long learning experience.

Although they are in retirement from their careers, the Brock House Writers continue to seek knowledge. The more they learn, the more they realize that there is so much more to learn, and the more excited they are about living each day.

LIFEWRITING

FOR ESL STUDENTS

"Human beings live to express themselves."

"You only become conscious of your own value when people listen to you."

Bishop James Mahoney

In the multicultural classrooms typical of most schools today, there will be some, perhaps even many, students who are either learning English as a second language or learning the language of the classroom as a second English dialect.

For ESL and ESD students mainstreamed into regular classes, the need for self-expression is probably even more important than for the rest of the class. They are students whose roles in the classroom may be marginalized because of communication difficulties or cultural differences.

These students need opportunities to develop their sense of self-identity and to express this self in the classroom in ways that other students will respond to and appreciate. They have many stories to share about their various cultural backgrounds and experiences. Giving them a chance to do so helps them reveal themselves as individuals unfettered by the stereotypical preconceptions of others.

However, ESL and ESD students may lack the English language skills needed to express their memories, feelings and ideas. Moreover, some of them may come from a culture in which this kind of expression of individuality is frowned upon. As a result, while introducing lifewriting to these students may be challenging, it is definitely worth the effort, especially in light of current thinking about teaching ESL.

Communicative Approaches to Teaching ESL

Gone are the days when second language students were confronted with countless grammar rules and word-for-word translation exercises. Less pervasive, too, is the audio-lingual approach that emphasized repeating patterns and contrastive analysis to work on the differences between the learner's native language and the target language. Today, we recognize that ESL students have already experienced one process of language learning by mastering their native language. Research shows that people learn a second language by a similar process.

Language learning programs based on the needs of the students suggest that they first learn the words and phrases necessary to survive in their new country. But the human need for social interaction requires that they also be able to express personal feelings and attitudes, shifting the emphasis toward communication and away from the drilling of set language patterns. A foundation of personal, expressive language helps meet this need and serves as a foundation for the more sophisticated language development required when tackling the structures and vocabulary students are expected to use in academic settings.

Research in the psycholinguistics of language acquisition also supports the view that children learn language interactively, rather than as passive receptors of the language forms given to them by adults. This means that the language learners must "try out" language to see if it works. They need to experiment with it in order to learn from their mistakes. They also need to create in their new language, feeling free to make mistakes without fear of recrimination, rather than being protected from supposedly "bad" linguistic habits.

Recognizing that the prime function of language is communication, classroom teachers of mainstreamed ESL students with some English competency can be guided by the axiom, "Fluency before accuracy." However, because these ESL students may be stigmatized by the obvious mistakes they make, it is sometimes difficult for teachers to resist trying to be helpful by correcting errors whenever possible. But people who find themselves corrected every time they open their mouths will soon stop talking altogether. "Fluency before accuracy" means that the teacher accepts the errors in the spontaneous language students use to communicate ideas and feelings, and responds sympathetically to what is being expressed, rather than focusing on the way it is expressed.

Finally, the current philosophy of language learning emphasizes that students learn most effectively in authentic situations, using materials that are relevant to their personal experience. The lifewriting unit, which draws primarily upon students' own experiences, certainly creates authentic situations. It gives students the opportunity to share with each other their life stories, their memories, their family histories, their opinions, their prejudices, their hopes and their fears in a classroom atmosphere of sympathy and tolerance. This is the very stuff of everyday human interaction.

Helping ESL Students

For both first and second language learners, the principle of the lifewriting program holds true: talking and writing go hand in hand. Talking is itself a means of generating and expanding ideas, and "talking writing" is the best means of getting feedback from a conference partner. But ESL students, because they lack proficiency in oral English, may be at a disadvantage during the idea-generating activities suggested earlier. Their recollections may come to mind first in their native language, and they may find it difficult to record them because of their limited knowledge of English vocabulary and idiom. Some students may find it necessary to translate rather than express ideas directly in English.

In basic ESL classes, the language experience approach, as represented by the following statements, has helped students make the jump from oral to written language.

If you experience something,
    You can talk about it, or
        You can act it, or
           You can draw it.
If you can communicate it,
    You can write it, or
        Someone can write it for you.
If it is written down,
    You can read it,
        And share it.

Using this approach, students dictate their ideas to the teacher who records them on a sheet of chart paper, the chalk-board or the computer screen. The ideas — and the words — are the students'. They own the text that the teacher records for them. They can then copy their story for themselves, and share it as a text for reading. The stories can be based on one student's experience or a collaborative effort stemming from a common experience, such as a field trip or Halloween party.

The language experience approach can be useful in a regular class as a confidence-builder for some students. Fortunately, the organization of the class as a writers' workshop allows the teacher the freedom to work with a small group while the rest of the students are engaged in composing their own stories. As well, some intervention by the teacher may be necessary to ensure that when students are engaged in peer conferences, the ESL students who need special help can work closely with a native speaker.

When the teacher is helping the whole class come up with ideas and memories as grist for future writing, she won't be able to offer ESL students very much individual attention. But she can assure them that they are free to get their ideas down on paper in whatever way works best for them. If, during a free writing session they cannot think of the English word they need, they can leave a space to be filled in later, or they can jot it down in their native language, knowing that they can look it up in a dictionary or get help translating it later. Problems with syntax can also be addressed later.

An idea-generating session may also be a good time to encourage vocabulary-building. Visual representation serves as an intermediate step between idea and word. Drawing and sketching scenes, characters, diagrams, maps and plans are acceptable ways of capturing ideas and memories. With the help of a dictionary or the support of someone who speaks English, these images can then be interpreted as written language that articulates the ideas they represent. The objects in a drawing can be labeled with their English names and dialogue balloons can be drawn to record the speech of characters included in sketches.

ESL students may also benefit from a series of sentence starters like the following that provide a syntactic framework to help them draw upon their memories, their cultural backgrounds, and their special abilities, including their ability to speak another language. Knowing that their mastery of another language is valued by the teacher and the class, ESL students gain confidence in their ability to learn another language, English.

— At home I speak....
— In my native language, "Hello" is..., "Goodbye" is..., "Please" is..., "Thank you" is....
— I used to live in..., but now I live in....
— What I like best about my native country is....
— What I like best about my new country is....
— School was different in my native country because....
— I am good at....
— I wish I could....

The best justification for using lifewriting with ESL students is that people learn most efficiently when the learning serves their immediate needs. There is no better motivation than the student's personal need to create a sense of self in the classroom, and this can be achieved by composing and sharing personal life stories and anecdotes.

No one should underestimate the power of emotional commitment in generating ideas that are important to the individual's sense of self. Many ESL students have lived through traumatic experiences; most have lived through the problem of moving from one country to another and from one culture to another. Lifewriting invites them to express these experiences, and the collaborative classroom gives them sympathetic listeners willing to respond to their stories.

The time allocated to collecting and drafting ideas is also a time when ESL learners can learn new words and idioms, either from the teacher or their peers, or from dictionaries, word-books, and the thesaurus. This is when the principle of fluency before accuracy really pays off. ESL students are encouraged to get their ideas down as best they can. Language errors can be identified and remedied before the work in progress goes on to the next draft. Difficulties with vocabulary, grammatical structures or idiomatic expressions can be addressed by the teacher or peer conference partners, with the ESL writer still in control of the story and able to incorporate suggestions for language improvement into the text. The ESL writer's need to get the language correct is satisfied when the story reaches the same standards for publication as those of the rest of the class. Although working through the process may take the ESL student longer, it is the successful outcome that counts.

The publication of a lifewriting story can be an important milestone in an ESL student's life — a sign that he or she has become accepted into a community of authors. The greatest gains in writing confidence and self-esteem come with the knowledge that the ESL writers in the classroom have become authors in the English language, and that their stories will be read and admired by others — the teacher, their peers and their parents.

Lifewriting for EFL Students

Students learning English as a foreign language in their home countries aren't usually immersed in an English-speaking environment as most ESL students are. They don't encounter many native English speakers at school, at home or through the media. The value of lifewriting for EFL students is illustrated by Sydney Butler's experiences when teaching four classes of Czech students at the Prague Institute of Chemical Technology during the heady, euphoric months after the "Velvet Revolution" and the fall of the Berlin Wall.

These technical students had some textbook knowledge of English gained through their academic study of English with Czech instructors who had used formal grammar instruction and translation methods. There had, however, been little contact with spoken English; Russian had been the required second language and the traditional second language was German.

The goal of the program was to develop the students' fluency in oral English so they could interact socially in this foreign language in the everyday world of a united Europe. Because few textbooks or other resources were available, the focus was on encouraging the students to use oral language to communicate among themselves. There were introductions, interviews, panel discussions, debates, reports on newspaper articles and sample dialogues around a number of themes, with a leavening of games, songs and improvised skits in which the students demonstrated their creativity.

By the third month, lifewriting had become part of the course almost inadvertently, as an extension of some oral sharing of personal stories. For the first lesson in this unit, the teacher had asked students to bring a photograph that showed something important in their lives. Most of them brought small black-and-white snapshots of family, pets, holiday excursions and student camping trips, all good material for sparking small-group conversations.

One difficulty was that some students did not have access to their family albums. With these students, the teacher improvised by providing small squares of plain paper, explaining that these were "do-it-yourself" snapshots. Students were invited to sketch any person, place or event in their life that they wished.

The actual drawing activity also proved to be an opportunity for rehearsing ideas and gathering words and idioms. The teacher normally helped each group collect the key words and phrases they would need in their conversations. For the students who were sketching their "snapshots," these words became labels for the drawings. Some students included dialogue in cartoon-like balloon attached to characters included in their sketches.

The life story conversations followed an established "jigsaw" pattern. Students from each group, having already composed and told their life stories, would visit other groups to show their pictures and repeat or extend their stories. All the students were encouraged to ask questions involving the five Ws — who, what, why, where and when — to help the storyteller elaborate on or clarify the story. This activity demonstrated the principle of the "communication gap": the storyteller had knowledge that the listeners did not.

This oral activity turned into lifewriting when some students began voluntarily writing out their complete stories as part of their preparation for storytelling. To some extent, they were driven by the desire to get the language right, even though the emphasis up to that point had been simply on communicating ideas. Correction of pronunciation, grammar and vocabulary was offered only if students were failing to get their message across. The overall goal of conveying meaning continued to take precedence over addressing difficulties with grammatical structures, common usage, and idiomatic expressions.

Once the stories were in written form, it was much easier to share them and give and receive suggestions for improving either the content or language usage. To give the revision process purpose, the teacher guaranteed to make a *samizdat* publication of the students' stories. Ultimately, a 56-page booklet was produced under the title "Stories from Prague: Lifestorying by Students at the Prague Institute of Chemical Technology." Forty-five Czech students became published authors in English. A sample story from this collection is shown here.

MY UNCONSCIOUS GOAL

I'll tell you about the danger about which I didn't know. Three years ago we played a soccer match . I was the striker. There was no score in the game, but ten minutes before the end I jumped at a ball to challenge with the goalie of our rivals. I was quicker that he and I headed the ball, and his hand struck my head. It was a knock out. I fell down in the grass and I lost consciousness.

The ambulance had come for me and took me to hospital. I woke up after an hour in the hospital. I forgot nothing. But round about me there were many of our players, and my coach, and they all had fear in their eyes. And they told me I scored the goal, and we won because of my goal.

Vasek

Vasek's drawing and story demonstrate the value of the activity in promoting a student's confidence in his ability to express a personal story in a second language. Vasek was cheerful and cooperative, but very shy about saying anything in English. Although his knowledge of the vocabulary and grammar was as good as any of the other students, he was very reluctant to participate in group conversations except as a listener. Nevertheless, his good humor overcame any possible sense of discouragement, and he maintained his interest in the class.

The breakthrough happened when the teacher asked the class to think about and list occasions when their lives or safety were threatened — accidents or sicknesses, or times when they felt afraid of a potential, rather than a real, danger. During the rehearsal time, Vasek produced the humorous drawing that accompanies his story and received some help from the teacher with a few key words and phrases.

The teacher also observed Vasek when his turn came to tell his story to his group. The other students were captivated by his drawing and listened attentively as he struggled through his retelling. This episode was the longest oral discourse that Vasek had ever attempted in the class, but he was able to achieve his goal, both figuratively and literally. He had actually communicated a real experience in English and his listeners had understood and appreciated his story, responding with smiles of approval.

The real value of the experience could be seen on Vasek's face, which reflected the glory of his achievement. To a large degree, his success depended on his personal involvement in the incident and his knowledge of the game that put him in the expert's seat. But he also experienced the joy of creativity because he had been able to construct a story with a delightful surprise ending. While it may have been a story he told often in his native Czech, this was the first time he had taken the trouble to shape it into a literary event. Vasek's immediate reward that day was to be chosen as his group's representative to visit the other groups, repeating and expanding his story before three other audiences. Their feedback may have motivated him to produce the written draft that eventually became part of the class booklet.

Like Vasek, all students — ESL, EDL, EFL and native English speaking — bring to the classroom a wealth of life experience and the creative talents that enable them to shape these experiences into satisfying, entertaining stories that can be enjoyed by responsive readers. Experiencing success with using English to express themselves may be even more important for students whose first language is not English than it is for native speakers. If non-native speakers feel confident of their ability to express themselves in their new language, it may help them overcome some of the problems of adjusting to a new home and a new culture.

TEACHER'S STORY: *Lifewriting in ESL Classes*

STEVE DUNBAR

The Vancouver School Board is currently sponsoring a writing project to develop an anthology of materials written by secondary ESL students for use in other ESL classes and in regular English and social studies courses. The purpose of the project is to provide ESL students with an opportunity to use process writing, or lifewriting, to improve their written communication by telling stories about their lives. A further purpose is to make the stories available to English-speaking students in order to give them a greater understanding of new immigrants to Canada, and to prepare a path for dialogue. This project is designed to reduce the social and linguistic isolation of ESL students.

As a participant in the project, I was curious to see what interest mainstream students would show in the writing of their ESL peers. As an example, I shared with my mainstream class a story written by a Taiwanese student that outlined how our system of education had not matched his expectations, which were formed by his school experiences in his native country. The head of our English department, who also presented this story to his class, reported on the value of making this link of understanding between ESL and students. He said that this kind of contact helps break down the barriers of shyness, ignorance or fear that may exist between the grade-level population and ESL students.

In our school, we've found that both mainstream and ESL students benefit from writing and sharing their personal stories with an audience interested in learning about their ideas and experiences and willing to overlook some imperfections in the surface conventions of written language. They are writing for themselves and their peers, not just for a teacher, who might be be concerned primarily with errors in spelling, verb tenses or paragraphing, and are gaining valuable experience in both writing and communicating.

The sharing of lifewriting stories has reduced the linguistic and cultural distance between English-speaking and ESL students. It has also benefited the school population in general by making greater use of the human resources available within the school. As we continue with this project, we expect that the ESL population will feel more confident about branching out from the security of their language and cultural peer groups to take a more active part in school life. At the same time, other students will have more opportunity to gain a better understanding of the fears and frustrations of the newest arrivals to our school and country.

. . . .

LIFEWRITING FOR ADULTS

"The only purpose of life is the creation of a self and what matters, finally, is the sum total of all one's attempts."

Gore Vidal

"Narrative is the study of how humans make meaning of experience by endlessly telling and retelling stories about themselves that both refigure the past and create purpose in the future."

Michael Connelly and Jean Clandenin

Adults don't usually require as extensive an introduction to lifewriting as younger students. Once the activity is explained, most adults are immediately interested. They have more to talk about, including opinions, judgments, and experiences that they may want to get out of their systems, and they are eager to talk and share their experiences. So, less motivation is required, and fewer introductory or lead-in activities.

This does not mean that teachers can eliminate all preliminary work. They should still present a clear description of the task and how the group is expected to proceed, and outline the agenda for each meeting, including the expected outcomes of or objectives for each session. They also need to organize the class into groups and make whatever changes might be needed in the physical layout to facilitate this type of work. As well, no matter how enthusiastic participants are about the oral activities and the class itself, they will still have some difficulty getting ideas down on paper and will need incentives to help them persist. These incentives could include assigning students certain tasks and responsibilities, ensuring that each person has a chance to shine brightly as the "star" of the class, providing hand-outs and demonstrations, and arranging "show-and-tell" activities and visits from "mystery guests."

Readings from the writing of previous students, a published autobiography or a newspaper or magazine can provide additional stimulation during each session. Whole-class discussions of topics like How Schools Have Changed, Things Were Better Then or What I Remember from My Pre-School Days are also effective in keeping participants talking among themselves. As long as they are doing so, it's a good idea for the teacher to remain in the background, giving directions only as needed. He should also hold off proposing changes or new challenges until students have actually begun to write.

It's worth noting that there's an especially good fit between the philosophical underpinnings of lifewriting reflected in the quotes at the beginning of this chapter and the expectations of most adults who enroll in the classes. Adults who sign up for programs offered as college, university or extension courses, or at places like community centers, libraries, seniors' recreation centers, retirement homes, women's centers and even prisons are usually looking for less formal, less competitive or less "evaluative" types of instruction. These are the settings where lifewriting programs are often given, and this is certainly the kind of instruction they provide. So, lifewriting activities tend to attract like-minded adults willing to focus on common goals — the sharing of stories and exploration of the self.

Motivation through Lifewriting

Adults interested in self-exploration are quickly drawn into lifewriting. Sharing their life stories with sympathetic listeners and readers prods their memory banks, and they are spurred on by the excitement that comes from bringing into consciousness more and more of what seemed to have been forgotten. They want to continue working through the satisfying processes of talking about their lives and telling their stories to the more difficult task of transforming the memories into writing.

Nowhere is this intrinsic drive toward self-realization and self-exploration more evident than in specialized centers such as prisons. Groups of seniors are usually equally driven, often expressing the desire to leave personal records or to contribute to a family history. Even students at the college or school level seeking to develop general English writing skills find that exploring the past provides an easy, interesting, and stimulating transition to more academically oriented forms of writing. The process is so engaging that after a time some students, seemingly unaware of the progress they are making in writing and revising, begin to worry about the lack of formal lessons on usage, grammar, and structure. Some may even begin to feel guilty about being involved in a series of interesting activities rather than in the skill development exercises they came prepared for, and they need to be reassured that these skills are indeed being addressed.

In the institutional setting, one may also find adult students looking for some version of literacy training or ESL instruction. The sharing of life stories and the collaborative approach work very well with them, as do the introductory activities of developing a word bank, and charting and producing lifelines. Word banks provide the bricks and lifelines the mortar in building a house of memories. No longer struggling to find an essay topic or a story plot, they can concentrate on first expressing the idea orally and then getting it into written form.

Chronicling a family history leads many adults to pursue lifewriting with a special tenacity. Initially, however, they do not have in mind an autobiographical record or a series of memoirs. What they envision is some sort of fact-book or chronology of events like births, marriages and deaths, or a family tree that includes dates and places inhabited by various branches of the family, as well as significant accomplishments of their kinfolk.

Although these purposes can be accommodated to some extent within a lifewriting program, it is well to remind people interested in endeavors like this that the direction of the class will be toward writing and self-exploration, not collecting data and producing charts, although family records may also provide a structure for the lifewriting that brings facts to life.

The Forms of Lifewriting

There is a narrow view of lifewriting that sees it solely as a reconstruction of what has happened to an individual, relegating to the background details or events that did not affect the writer directly. But, with the benefit of forgetfulness and the editing power of hindsight, what inevitably emerges is a sort of fictionalized reality rather than an objectively true chronicle of events and feelings. However, attempts to confine lifewriting by drawing fine distinctions between one form and another should not bother us. Once we understand that we are never recapturing the "true story" of what happened, we are set free to search out the emotional truth or the retrospective truths of the past if we so wish. And although some purists might say, for instance, that memoirs are not true autobiography, in lifewriting all such variations in genre are accommodated.

Still, a fairly traditional autobiographical approach is an effective way to begin priming the memory pump. A simple outline like the following will certainly get people thinking and talking very quickly.

My family

Grandparents
Parents
Siblings
Spouse
Children
Places where my family has lived

My life so far

Pre-school, earliest memories
Schools
Activities, interests
Special occasions, events, trips, visitors
Employment

My future

Expectations, ambitions, hopes
Fantasies

Once adults have begun writing their own life stories, some of them may use these beginnings to structure a full-scale autobiography, and their lifewriting can become a series of autobiographical sketches designed to encompass their lives to date. Others might work on a memoir, vignette or a series of adventures. Diaries and letters, which tend to take the shape of random recollections rather than a sequential accounting, are other possible forms.

In our view of lifewriting, there are no carved-in-stone rules defining the form the vehicle should take, just as there is no inherent obligation to present only the factual. The truth, as in *le pacte autobiographique*, is the truth of self-representation, and it can be found even in autobiographical fiction, in which the self becomes a character created by a third-person narrator.

All autobiographical genres, as well as short stories and anecdotes, poems and ballads, dialogues, short plays, conversations, photo essays, art essays and videos, are worthy of exploration in the lifewriting program. The lifewriter will choose the form and style for a piece of writing according to what seems most suitable for the material, with the understanding that what the audience expects is a central figure who tells about the people, places, events, turning points or beliefs in a life well-examined.

The Themes of Lifewriting

A number of themes emerge as central to adult lifewriting. First, there are the themes of childhood reconsidered. These memories become stronger as one ages, and often the events are clearer and carry more meaning than seemingly more important career accomplishments. With vivid memories of a trip, of being lost, of some small success or failure, of a pet or a favorite toy, of fights with friends and siblings, or of a special hiding place, the focus is often on a growing awareness of their significance.

Second, there are the themes of adolescence centered on an increasing awareness of the world in general, with particular attention being paid to the importance of peers and best friends, sexual attractions, feelings of independence expressed in rebellion, and favorite hobbies and sports. Recollections of adolescence also draw to the surface an emerging view of parents as people with their own foibles, and first articulations of life ambitions.

Entry into adulthood, so often vividly recalled from the distance of maturity, is a third theme frequently woven through adults' lifewriting. Recurring topics are frequently traumatic — making a break from family by leaving home, marrying, getting a job in another city, and so on. This is the time when many of our life-forming decisions are made, and looking back is often tinged with feelings of regret for the road not taken. For mature lifewriting participants, there is an opportunity to put the world in focus, to see things anew, to settle old scores, to right old wrongs. In fact, it has been suggested that for adult participants lifewriting comes to mean "life righting."

The Lifewriting Resource Kit

For the factually oriented lifewriter involved in a longer-term program of life review, a lifewriting resource kit provides endless opportunities for activities that build and maintain enthusiasm by turning up a continuing series of topics for reflection, talking, sharing and writing. Indeed, the kit itself becomes an artifact of the program. The easiest way to organize the kit is in a portable cardboard legal-size filing box, using about a dozen file folders to start. The task is to assemble items that can fit into general categories.

For example, the Family Background file may contain materials such as a family Bible, old photographs, the family tree, old house deeds, wills, bills, heirlooms and newspaper clippings. The Childhood file may hold birth announcements, awards, drawings, baby pictures and even treasured picture books, stories and nursery rhymes. The Education file might include old school books, certificates, report cards, class pictures, awards and school magazines. The Employment file will hold records of employment like old résumés, application forms, pay slips, and trade or professional journals. A Travel or Entertainment file can hold tickets, menus, hotel brochures and pamphlets, theater or concert ticket stubs, postcards and itineraries. The Home Business file will take care of diaries, bills, product guarantees, insurance policies, mortgage documents, bank records and income tax returns. A Friendship file might hold personal correspondence, postcards and pictures. Marriage, Children, and Grandchildren files can also be assembled.

There may also be an assortment of objects and mementos as well as paper and photographic records. Gathering and sorting this material will evoke ideas and memories; sharing it with others who are making similar collections will invite comparisons; and revisiting it from time to time will stimulate new lifewriting ideas.

Lifelines

A less arduous beginning can be made by using a simple lifeline — a line drawn across a blank page or a large sheet of drawing paper. This line can be marked off into life stages: family background, childhood, adolescence, adulthood, and maturity. These titles provide the pegs on which the lifewriters can hang their memories by recording names, keywords, phrases, dates, places, addresses, telephone numbers and so on. The value of this process is that each jotting seems to jog more and more memories. The exploration can be deepened by adding one or two parallel timelines — one for local events, another for world events — that will provide the broader contexts for the individual memories. The use of history books and old newspapers and magazines provides a backdrop of reality to the individual memories. A fascinating field trip for a small class is a visit to the local library where participants can search the newspaper files to find out what made local, national, or international news on the day they were born, or other significant dates.

The social aspects of sharing and collaboration motivate participants to bring in a wealth of information unearthed in the recesses of memory, home and archives. That motivation also eases them into the transition from idle remembering through to focused telling and on to reflective writing. Like Sequoia, the Cherokee chief, who watched the American soldiers being "talked to" by their books and letters and then "talking back" onto blank paper, they want others to hear their voices when they are not present and to speak to others over a distance. To do this, Sequoia had to learn how to "talk" Cherokee to the paper, a process that involved creating his own Cherokee alphabet by analyzing the sounds of his own language.

Of course, today's lifewriters need not match the intensity of Sequoia's motivation and commitment. The alphabet is already there for the using, and the lifewriting process is available to them too. What's more, whether the adult life-writer is a competent fluent writer, a person learning English, or someone determined to improve basic literacy skills, the lifewriting program also makes some guarantees. It delivers on promises of social benefits that come from sharing with others in the group, of a sense of self-identity through the expression of personal ideas, and of the feelings of self-worth that result from the appreciation of sympathetic listeners and readers.

Lifewriting also guarantees success. Some writers may take longer than others; some may need more help from the teacher and their peers. But eventually everyone can compose and write a life story. Most groups will be reassured at the beginning of the process by this aphoristic restating of the language experience approach to learning: If you can think of a story, you can tell the story; if you can tell the story, you can write the story; if you can write the story, then others can read it — and like Sequoia, your voice can be heard over time and over space.

Finally, in planning sessions for adult groups, the teacher should ensure that there is always time for social interaction. The following sample plan includes a balanced combination of text reading, general talk, and idea-generating activities as the basis for short periods of quiet time when participants are alone with their thoughts and motivated to get their ideas down on paper.

A Basic Plan for a Two-hour Session

1. Introduction and Warm-up (10 minutes)
   The leader reads from her own story, or from a published source.
2. General Sharing (45 minutes)
   Each participant is given the opportunity to read or tell about the story composed in the previous meeting.
3. Break (10 minutes)
   Participants may continue to share stories with a partner.
4. New Stories (15 minutes)
   Leader introduces a new memory key or theme; participants note ideas that pertain to their own lives; with a partner, each person tells the story that is going to be written.

113

5. Idea Generation (15 minutes)
   Participants focus on the topic for their new stories, while the leader takes them through a heuristic activity to generate more ideas.
6. Quiet Writing Time (15 minutes)
   The leader offers individual help when needed, or writes her own story.
7. Conclusion (10 minutes)
   General discussion on the success of the activity. Individual commitment to finish the draft of a story for the next class, and to be ready to share by telling or reading the story.

It's worth noting that leader-directed activity occupies only 35 minutes of this plan out of a total of 120 . For two-thirds of the session, the participants are in control, expressing and sharing their own ideas.

Motivated by interest or curiosity, adults come to lifewriting programs by choice, not necessity. They come not to be taught but to learn, not to sit but to do. They come to sharpen their wits by interacting with others, and they want to leave feeling that they have enjoyed themselves while being challenged intellectually. During and at the end of the session, leaders should ask themselves:: "Will their engagement in this class be enough to bring them back again?" The number who return is a measure of the program's success.

TEACHER'S STORY: *Lifewriting in an Adult Literacy Program*

KEN RIDLEY

For four years, I had the pleasure of tutoring students in an adult basic education program at a community college. Some of the students were learning English as a second language; others were native speakers who had problems with reading and writing. My main concern was the improvement of their written English.

With the agreement and cooperation of the instructor, I decided to use lifewriting techniques in order to publish a monthly booklet of the students' own stories. Previously, the students had been asked to write standard exercises based upon a set of pictures or to write practice sentences and to correct errors. Lifewriting produced startlingly different results.

Before, we had been fortunate to get a paragraph or two at the most from any of the students. Most of them were reluctant to write anything at all, and their writing was stilted and unimaginative. With lifewriting, we began to get stories of three or four pages written with intense feeling. Standards of grammar or spelling did not improve, but the students' feeling that something was being accomplished in their writing improved tremendously. For the first time, they felt that they had something important to say in their writing. They were highly motivated and excited by producing real stories. They wanted others to know of their feelings and experiences.

I used a variety of lead-in topics about which the students could express their own opinions. One popular topic was Heroes. And because the students were keen to become productive members of the work force, the topic My First Job also got them talking and writing. Eventually, this activity became a sort of job search, as the students used their writing to explore their hopes and goals for employment.

· · · · · · · · · · · · · · ·

LIFEWRITING FOR TEACHERS

"Our precommitment about the nature of life is that it is a story, some narrative however incoherently put together."

Jerome Bruner

"For many students, perhaps all, a primary object of attention and interest is the self."

Robert J. Graham

Innovative teachers are always on the lookout for new ideas that might benefit their students, but are often so busy that they pass over ideas that might help them personally as teachers. But lifewriting in the classroom draws teachers as well as students into the process. They are writing when their students are writing, and they share their work with the students too. Having become involved in the process in this way, they may find it very beneficial to use lifewriting as a means of reflecting further on their personal lives, teaching experiences and professional goals. They may also wish, by way of professional development, to take a closer look at some of the educational philosophies behind our approach to lifewriting and to explore the possibilities of extending the boundaries of lifewriting far beyond the classroom.

Extending the Boundaries

As we've already said many times, our use of the term "lifewriting" can include formal autobiography, but we believe that people can be overpowered by the thought of producing a true autobiography. Surely a work like this is a full-fledged book, a telling of a complete life lived by a person whose deeds and accomplishments are so significant that they merit such impressive treatment, publication and readership? As well as feeling overwhelmed by the genre and "unworthy" of star billing in a self-generated work, most amateur writers cannot sustain the effort required to complete such a task.

On the other hand, everyone can achieve some level of lifewriting as we see it, especially if the process is made easier and more attractive by offering group support and by focusing on particular events or incidents that can be written about in one sitting. And it may very well be that enough of these tiny gems could be strung together one day to become an actual autobiography. That's a possibility held out to all lifewriters.

The broader view of lifewriting also encompasses many other genres, and acts as a magnet for accounts or retellings that do not fit tidily into any literary genre. It can take under its wing such personal stories as court testimonies, obituaries, collections of letters, edited journals and diaries, or even family Christmas letters and gardening records.

Clearly then, lifewriting recognizes and celebrates so-called alternative texts. For example, it has given a necessary prominence to often-ignored feminist writings and feminist interpretations of history. As Marlene Kadar noted in her collection of essays on lifewriting, "The literary history of autobiography has also been a womanless history, whereas life writing offers a feminist canon, among others." Freed of the narrow perceptions of lifewriting as a historical record, practitioners can engage in something approaching "life righting" — an attempt to restructure experience, to find cause-and-effect in one's life, to place oneself in one's mind back into society, and to gain some measure of control over life. A recognition of the importance of doing this may underlie the increasing visibility in various media of heretofore marginalized groups — women, aboriginals, racial minorities, gays and lesbians, immigrants, various ethnic groups and the working classes — as they come forward with their own interpretations of history and contemporary society. Lifewriting offers them a variety of forms of expression that are immediately accessible to all.

Our view of lifewriting also recognizes that there are many ways other than through writing to manifest life stories. Sometimes a person can trace a life through the pages of a photograph album, or by reviewing old 8-mm home movies. Videotape is a contemporary medium for recording life events with the ubiquitous camcorder, and as the editing process becomes easier and less costly, will even permit the blending of recorded interviews that give the subject's oral life stories some permanence.

Drawing and painting may also be seen as a form of life review. In Margaret Atwood's *Cat's Eye*, the main character, Elaine, is an artist whose retrospective show provides a series of visual images that reflect the structure of her life already told in the words of the novel. In a similar vein, music — composed or played by an individual, or remembered as a collection of recorded pieces marking the major passages of life — can be used as a form of life review.

These, and many other approaches, can be used as preliminaries to the actual writing, but they can also stand alone or be part of a multi-media presentation.

An Educational Context

There is ample justification for using lifewriting in the English classroom. The approach was well-documented in a landmark research project a quarter-century ago described in *Language and Learning*.

In setting out these ideas in an article titled "Their Language and Our Teaching," James Britton concluded that "the area in which language operates in English lessons is that of personal experience, in other words, relations with other people, the identity of the individual, the relations between the ego and the environment."

In his view of a student-centered education Britton shows that it is necessary for the pupil to create a personal context for all curricular content, and that the medium for so personalizing knowledge is "expressive speech" — the language that is close to the self of the speaker.

In *The Development of Writing Abilities*, Britton stresses the place of the expressive mode in both oral and written language as the means of learning in general:

> Not only is it the mode in which we approach and relate to each other in speech, but it is also the mode in which, generally speaking, we frame the tentative first drafts of new ideas: and the mode in which, in times of family or national crisis, we talk with our own people and attempt to work our way towards some kind of resolution. By

analogy with these roles in speech, it seemed likely to us that expressive writing might play a key role in a child's learning. It must surely be the most accessible form in which to write, since family conversation will have provided him with a familiar model. Furthermore, a writer who envisages his reader as someone with whom he is on intimate terms must surely have very favorable conditions for using the process of writing as a means of exploration and discovery.

Teachers may find the work of Robert Graham particularly interesting, because his study of autobiography in education and the curriculum is firmly based on the epistemology of John Dewey's social construction of knowledge:

> The students' self might be considered an object of inquiry or experiment, hence turning the writing of autobiography and autobiographical discourses into a way of thinking, a conceptual instrument of cognition.

In Graham's view, autobiographical writing enables students to observe, perceive, interact and reflect on the world, so that both the affective and cognitive factors of human consciousness coalesce in an expression of the value or interest that knowledge holds for the self:

> For many students, perhaps all, a primary object of attention and interest is the self; and to construct the self means to pursue the consequences of inquiry or active experimentation into or on that self, to discover how it has evolved and how it is situated or might be situated in society. The autobiographical impulse to write the self, as well as providing access to the forms of knowledge, supplies the warrant for providing and pursuing those autobiographical activities mentioned before that were designed to engage the student in the process of constructing and reconstructing the self in language.

Teachers' Stories

Finally, lifewriting holds value for us as teachers constantly engaged in planning and revising programs and instructional methods. Just as autobiographically grounded writing provides students with access to knowledge of the world, so too the stories we tell as teachers may enable us to better understand our classrooms, our students, and the learning that takes place. In other words, lifewriting can become a key to curriculum planning as our personal narratives help us to discern the past and plan for the future.

In his study of life as narrative, Jerome Bruner showed how our life stories can become the foundation for life planning:

> The ways of telling and the ways of conceptualizing that go with them become so habitual that they finally become recipes for structuring experience itself, for laying down routes into memory, for not only guiding the life narrative up to the present but directing it into the future.

Michael Connelly and Jean Clandinin take this concept into the teacher's professional field by establishing "the legitimacy of each teacher's personal knowledge of classrooms" through the "telling and retelling of stories about our past" as a way of working out "new ways of acting in the future." They see storytelling as an essentially human activity:

Narrative is the study of how humans make meaning of experience by endlessly telling and retelling stories about themselves that both refigure the past and create purpose in the future.

In Connelly and Clandinin's view, education is a "a narrative of experience that grows and strengthens a person's capabilities to cope with life." They discuss a number of reflective writing tools to help teachers recover their "personal knowledge," including journals, biography, picturing, telling stories of themselves as teachers, interviews of teachers and letter-writing between colleagues. Their analysis of teachers' stories demonstrates how narratives embody "beliefs, values and action preferences," providing the basis for curriculum development, planning and implementation. Through our narratives of experiences we derive our "personal practical knowledge" that becomes our personal curriculum and a "metaphor for understanding students' curriculum."

To put this theory into practice, teachers may wish to try their hand at lifewriting stimulated by the following explorations that we have used when conducting workshops for teachers.

A Memorable Teacher

Which teachers do you remember?
Who was the kindest? The most demanding? The most knowledgeable? The most encouraging?
Who taught you the most valuable lessons?
Describe your most memorable teacher. List the qualities that made that teacher outstanding.

A Memorable Moment in Teaching and Learning

Focus on a particular incident in your education, either as a student or a teacher. Are there "Eureka!" moments of revelation, or a more gradual change in perception? Is there a moment when you decided to become a teacher? What or who led you to choose your particular vocation?

The Teacher I Would Like to Be

What is your potential as a teacher? What are your strengths? In which areas would you like to improve? What has been your most successful teaching experience? How will your ex-students talk about you in the future?

My Happiest Memory as a Teacher

What classes, lessons, schools or situations have given you the most satisfaction? What are your most memorable encounters with students? What would be your ideal teaching situation?

A Day When Things Went Wrong

Elementary teachers often use Judith Viorst's *Alexander and the Terrible, Horrible, No-good, Very Bad Day* as a model for their students' emergent writing. You can use it as a model for exorcising the teaching demons that may plague your life.

Stories generated by these lifewriting ideas may already be the stuff of classroom conversations. In written form they have additional value because they can be preserved and shared with colleagues to create a dialogue about teaching experiences and philosophies — a dialogue that is likely to enhance our future practices.

In both the creating and the sharing, lifewriting provides teachers with opportunities to reflect on themselves and their teaching practices. Appreciating the limitations of empirical findings, we have moved towards valuing other forms of knowledge, including personal knowledge. For example, many faculties of education accept the use of educational autobiography as an approach to writing a graduate thesis.

In fact, at every level of education, lifewriting is both appropriate and pertinent, because it promotes both an exploratory and a reflective attitude to experience. The "learning place" described by Carl Leggo in an article in *Crossroads and Horizons in Teacher Education* provides a vision of a school as a place that welcomes personal expression:

> (It is) primarily a place for gathering together to explore experiences of the world, to discuss what is being learned about life, a place for sharing and growing, a place for experimentation, a place for trying on disguises, and playing with the letters of the alphabet, and considering the mistakes and successes of the historical past, and conjecturing about the mistakes and successes of the imagined future, a place for examining the dynamic and processes and influences which shape the lived experiences of being human and becoming human.

For both teachers and students alike, lifewriting can make schools a welcoming place.

. . . .

BIBLIOGRAPHY

Bentley, R. & S. Butler. *Lifewriting: Self-Exploration and Life Review through Writing*. Dubuque, Iowa: Kendall/Hunt, 1988.

Britton, J. *Language and Learning*. Harmondsworth, England: Penguin, 1970.

Britton, J. "Their Language and Our Teaching." In *English in Education*. Vol. 4, no. 2: 1970.

Britton, J. *The Development of Writing Abilities*. London: Macmillan, 1975.

Bruner, J.S. "Research Currents: Life as Narrative." In *Language Arts*. Vol. 65, no. 6: 1988.

Bullock, A.L.C.A. *A Language for Life: Report of the Committee of Inquiry Appointed by the Secretary of State for Education and Science under the Chairmanship of Sir Allen Bullock*. London: Her Majesty's Stationery Office, 1975.

Buss, H.M. "Anna Jameson's *Winter Studies and Summer Rambles in Canada* as Epistolary Dijournal." In *Essays on Life Writing: From Genre to Critical Practice*. (Marlene Kadar, Ed.) Toronto: University of Toronto Press, 1992.

Butler, S. & R. Bentley. "Lifewriting Is Writing Self-Possessed." In *Priorities 7*. Australian Education Network, 1995.

Butler, S. & R. Bentley. "Literacy through Lifewriting: The Foundation of Growth in Engagement." In *English Quarterly*. Vol. 24, no. 3-4: 1992.

Connelly, F.M. & D.J. Clandinin. *Teachers as Curriculum Planners: Narratives of Experience.* New York: Teachers College Press, Columbia University, 1988.

Elbow, P. *Writing without Teachers.* New York: Oxford University Press, 1973.

Graham, R.J. *Reading and Writing the Self: Autobiography in Education and the Curriculum.* New York: Teachers College Press, Columbia University, 1988.

Hairston, M. "The Winds of Change: Thomas Kuhn and the Revolution in the Teaching of Writing." In *College Composition and Communication.* Vol. 33, no. 1: 1982.

Holt, John. *The Underachieving School.* New York: Pitmans, 1969.

Kadar, M. (Ed.). *Essays on Life Writing: From Genre to Critical Practice.* Toronto: University of Toronto Press, 1992.

Leggo, C. "A Reflection on Narrative and Community in Teacher Education." In *Crossroads and Horizons in Teacher Education: Proceedings of the Westcast, 1992, Conference.* (L. Beauchamp et al., eds.) Edmonton: University of Alberta, 1993.

Moffett, J. *Teaching the Universe of Discourse.* Boston: Houghton Mifflin, 1968.

Murray, D.M. "All Writing Is Autobiography." In *College Composition and Communication.* Vol. 42, no. 1: 1991.

Rosen, H. *Stories and Their Meanings.* Sheffield, England: National Association of Teachers of English, 1984.

Wixon, V. & P. Stone. "Getting It Out, Getting It Down: Adapting Zoellner's Talk-Write." In *English Journal.* Vol. 69, no. 6: 1977.

MORE TITLES FROM THE PIPPIN TEACHER'S LIBRARY

Helping Teachers Put Theory into Practice

STORYWORLDS: LINKING MINDS AND IMAGINATIONS
THROUGH LITERATURE
Marlene Asselin, Nadine Pelland, John Shapiro
Using literature to create rich opportunities for learning.

WHOLE LANGUAGE: PRACTICAL IDEAS
Mayling Chow, Lee Dobson, Marietta Hurst, Joy Nucich
*Down-to-earth suggestions for both shared and independent reading
and writing, with special emphasis on evaluation strategies.*

THE WHOLE LANGUAGE JOURNEY
Sara E. Lipa, Rebecca Harlin, Rosemary Lonberger
*Making the transition to a literature-based, child-centered
approach to learning.*

WRITING PORTFOLIOS:
A BRIDGE FROM TEACHING TO ASSESSMENT
Sandra Murphy, Mary Ann Smith
*How portfolios can help students become active partners
in the writing process.*

THE FIRST STEP ON THE LONGER PATH:
BECOMING AN ESL TEACHER
Mary Ashworth
*Practical ideas for helping children who are learning
English as a second language.*

SUPPORTING STRUGGLING READERS
Barbara J. Walker
*Building on struggling readers' strengths to help them broaden
their strategies for making sense of text.*

ORAL LANGUAGE FOR TODAY'S CLASSROOM
Claire Staab
*Integrating speaking and listening into the curriculum to help
children discover the power of language.*

AN EXCHANGE OF GIFTS:
A STORYTELLER'S HANDBOOK
Marion V. Ralston
*Imaginative activities to enhance language programs
by promoting classroom storytelling.*

THE WORD WALL: TEACHING VOCABULARY
THROUGH IMMERSION
Joseph Green

*Using mural dictionaries—word lists on walls—to strengthen
children's reading, speaking and writing skills.*

INFOTEXT: READING AND LEARNING
Karen M. Feathers

*Classroom-tested techniques for helping students overcome
the reading problems presented by informational texts.*

WRITING IN THE MIDDLE YEARS
Marion Crowhurst

*Suggestions for organizing a writing workshop approach
in the classroom.*

AND THEN THERE WERE TWO:
CHILDREN AND SECOND LANGUAGE LEARNING
Terry Piper

*Insights into the language-learning process help
teachers understand how ESL children become bilingual.*

IN ROLE: TEACHING AND LEARNING DRAMATICALLY
Patrick Verriour

*A leading drama educator demonstrates how easily drama can be used
to integrate learning across the curriculum.*

LINKING MATHEMATICS AND LANGUAGE: PRACTICAL
CLASSROOM ACTIVITIES
Richard McCallum, Robert Whitlow

*Practical, holistic ideas for linking language—both reading
and writing—and mathematics.*

TEACHING THE WORLD'S CHILDREN
Mary Ashworth, H. Patricia Wakefield

*'ors and primary teachers can help
gsters use—and learn—English.*

G GUIDE TO COMPREHENSION

*students to interact with,
ormation they read.*